HOW TO MANAGE YOUR BOSS

D1234752

HOW TO MANAGE YOUR BOSS

Raymond Monbiot

SCOPE BOOKS

First impression March 1980

All rights reserved. No part of this publication may be reproduced, stored in a retrieval system, or transmitted in any form or by any means, electronic, mechanical, photocopying, recording or otherwise, without permission in writing from the publisher.

© Scope Books 1980
3 Sandford House, Kingsclere,
Newbury, Berkshire RG15 8PA

British Library Cataloguing in Publication Data

Monbiot, Raymond
How to manage your boss.
1. Promotions – Anecdotes, facetiae, satire, etc.
2. Executives – Anecdotes, facetiae, satire, etc.
I. Title
658.4'07'142 HF5549.5.P7

ISBN 0 906619 04 1
ISBN 0 906619 05 X Pbk

Cover design and illustrations – Roland Chadwick.

Printed in England
Signland Limited, Farnham, Surrey

HF
5549.5
P7
M65

CONTENTS

Preface

For over 20 years I worked for an International Group, starting as a production trainee at the age of 18 and rising through sales, marketing and distribution to be Managing Director of a succession of subsidiary companies. In that period of time I worked for or came into contact with a succession of bosses, ranging from the deadbeat to the dynamic, with most shades in between.

There is no shortage of books, theory and courses on managing subordinates and getting on with colleagues, but I have yet to find any which deal satisfactorily with managing those above us. The assumption is, presumably, that there is little one can do in that exalted direction and that one must work in whatever atmosphere is created. Such a missing link in forging one's career is not to be accepted. In the pages that follow I offer my experiences in tackling this intriguing challenge. Doing one's job effectively and with imagination is the key to success in employment, but it cannot be done without an environment which brings out the best effort and least distraction. Your boss has a big part to play in establishing this atmosphere, whether it is one of creative thrust or political infighting, punitive restraint or expansive excitement.

Many highly competent people never settle down to achieve their potential or their goals because they spend too much of their time in conflict with and reacting to their bosses. This drives them out from job to job in a constant quest for freedom which they never find. Or it ties them down to jobs from which they get little satisfaction. A man's job should be his springboard and not his refuge.

Some of the stories I have written are apocryphal and any attempt to identify the characters would be a waste of time. All are drawn from real life in terms of experience and there is glory or scars to prove it. For 10 years I was a visiting lecturer at the College of Marketing, and those who attended the courses have provided interesting opportunities for observation. I have also been involved in the British Institute of Management, where there is so much still to do, and in voluntary work of all sorts, which provides rich material for observing life and the motivations of people. Not the least source of my material has been the time I spent as Chairman of a Conservative Parliamentary Constituency Association with one of the most interesting Cabinet Ministers as Member, and the chance to work with all sorts of people one would not normally meet in business.

I reckon I have seen or worked for a fair cross section of bosses. It has been a source of continual interest to observe and understand each of them so that performance in the job was freed from much of the blockage and frustration which cause anxieties and poor results. There has been conflict, but for the most part it has been the healthy conflict of ideas resulting in the stimulus to find a better solution. This is much to be preferred to the conflict of behaviour which sours the atmosphere and breeds hostility and bloody-mindedness. There have been a number of traumatic events which have led to confrontation and then action at a time of my choosing, and there have been good times too.

Three of my bosses stand out as exceptional. One of these for whom I worked for four years forged a view of business which combined energy, enterprise and toughness. He stretched and excited the imagination in a way which no-one else had done for me up to that time. There were moments when I cursed him for the hard driver he was, but there was never a time when I did not respect him. He was a good and lasting influence and now lives in Spain. My last boss in that Group was the second really outstanding man to whom I reported directly. His own capacity for work is phenomenal.

He would quest and probe until he was satisfied that you knew what you were doing, and then would give you every encouragement to get on with the job, with his backing always available. The more you revealed, the less he interfered.

My present boss completes the trio. He creates the atmosphere of expansive, open, exciting management where the prime preoccupation is pursuing, and achieving, clear objectives with integrity and his wholehearted support. There is a basic seeking after truth which cuts out so much of the diversion and bad practice which I have described in this book. These three set the high point of the landscape.

The good manager will pick his company if dynasty, tradition or perhaps location does not get in the way. He is not an indentured slave to be shoved around by whatever boss fate sends him. Yet he can do a good deal to manage his boss in any company, and the harmony or otherwise he achieves will determine his own success as few other factors can. It is to this pursuit that I invite you to turn . . . . . .

JUMP!
how high sir?
yes Mr Hugh
In which direction Mr Hugh?
immediately...

1. The Pecking Order

There has been a major shift in the business pecking order since the 1930s, and most companies have readjusted to this reality with some pain.

Fifty years ago the presence of a father figure, usually the owner/manager, led to a system where instructions came from above and obedience was demanded on pain of dismissal right through the organisation. The atmosphere of threat and discipline was reinforced by hungry dole queues and the prospect of real hardship if you lost your job. The tyranny was tempered by kindness, a sense of belonging and security as a reward for obedience and loyalty.

An owner boss might well cause an employee to worry himself to the point of illness and then, noticing for the first time that one of his 'family' was sick, would insist on his taking a holiday with a cheque for spending money. Some, having been the cause of an employee going sick, would appear with baskets of fruit and messages for a speedy recovery.

Yet there was much to be said for close contact with the man who owned the business. Direct communication between management and shop floor was possible without layers of management and experts, filters and interpreters getting in the way. Managers performed duties which were later split into separate jobs for experts. Decisions could be obtained without committees or a lengthy process of paper work. In fact, business was a good deal simpler.

Many of our great businesses were built up in this way where the family atmosphere and the strong-willed owner set the tone. They relied to a large extent on one proprietor or on a small number of related or closely associated proprietors. Marks and Spencer, Unilever, Great Universal Stores, Fords, Lyons, Sainsburys and many more all started with a man's invention or idea which grew to become an established part of our lives. The founding fathers gave life and a way of life to their businesses, and those who worked in them were aware of their presence and personalities.

The history of such companies abounds with legends and stories of memorable eccentricities. One member of the founding family of a company known to every household in the country was looking out of his office window and saw a man leaning against a wall doing nothing. He rushed out of his office down into the yard to confront this idleness –

"What are you doing?" he demanded.

"Waiting" was the reply.

"Waiting? Well, you can wait in your own time. Take this chit to the Treasury, get your money and go".

The next day the same man was leaning against the same wall and this time the boss sent for him.

"Did I speak to you yesterday?"

"Yes".

"Did you go and get that money at the Treasury?"

"Yes".

"Then why are you still here?"

"Well you see, Guv'ner, I don't work for your company, I work for Carter Paterson".

As business became more complex, so the external demands of Trade Associations, Unions and Government legislation pulled the attention of the boss outwards, at the very time he should have been concentrating on the business itself. This caused a vacuum which had to be filled, and in came the specialists and experts. Also, as businesses increased in size and complexity and the patriarchs died or released the reins, the need for these specialists from the outside world was acknowledged, sometimes belatedly. This brought pain to long serving and loyal survivors who saw their family circle invaded by managers who had grown up with different

TRADE ASSO
UNION
Back in 2 weeks boys
they'll take their orders from ME
from ME
I'll fix you kids'n
Boss, where are you?

values, and whose attitudes to the established custom and pecking order were irreverent and challenging at best, and quite possibly destructive.

Furthermore, in the late 1950s the supply of goods had at last caught up with demand, and new mass production methods and expanding technology meant greater attention must be paid to areas of market expertise. The Marketing Men flourished in soap powder and margarine businesses and then moved out to offer their services to other businesses whose sales were falling behind their production capacity. Too often companies grasped at this fashionable solution to their problem and allowed a twenty-eight-year-old marketing man, whose management experience had perhaps extended to a secretary and an assistant, to be positioned as the only shield from going out of business.

Many businesses discovered that although the ideas and solutions peddled by the marketing men pushed the company into doing what it was believed the consumer wanted, these experts were unable to pull together the people in the business and harness their enthusiasm to a new goal, because man management and leadership was beyond their experience. It is the problem which faces many graduates from business schools. They need to have had some basic supervision and management experience before they spend two years obtaining a master's degree in business administration. For when they have completed their degree course their expectation of salary and their belief in their worth to industry are so high that it would be wholly undesirable to entrust them with management of people for the first time on a scale to justify such a salary.

Managers must pursue two careers. Firstly, they must acquire expertise in some branch of business such as sales, finance or production, and then in management which is common to all. Management implies leadership and leadership implies a goal which all can understand and aim for. If you are a good manager you should be able to manage anything, because one of your characteristics will be that you surround yourself with people who are better than you at technical aspects of the job.

An expert or specialist who has no man management

experience will usually try to prove he is better at his job than those who work for him. If he does, he is destined for a lonely and salutary lesson while those who could help him stand and watch. Tolerance is not a marked quality of youth and in the late 50s and early 60s there were for the most part only young marketing men. As this was the expertise which industry lacked at a time of particular need, the pendulum lurched down the age and experience scale and left considerable pain and confusion in its wake.

This emphasis on one part of the business caused a new pecking order where the latest expert was the new saviour. The danger lay not only in puffing the importance of one individual or department, but in the fact that those other managers or departments which were not 'in' were 'out'. By the time the marketing manager had increased the business overheads, committed a new high level of advertising and proved he did not have an easy answer to the business's problems, he would have lost his glamour and the firm would be looking elsewhere for a solution. The Marketing Department then gave way to another, maybe management services, financial or technical, and the process of high hopes and inevitable disillusionment would start all over again. This 'Flavour of the Month' management was bound to cause problems.

By this time the atmosphere would be somewhat sour, with 'older' departments fighting stiff rearguard actions and younger and recently recruited managers condemning most people older than themselves and competing with their contemporaries. The favoured department can be guaranteed to cause acute suspicion and misery in the company. The fact that one manager spends a disproportionate amount of time with the chief executive gives rise to suspicion and jealousy. Those excluded from the meetings conclude that it is their own department or future which, along with everyone else's is being discussed and decided.

The old guard would go to considerable lengths to ensure their continued relationship with the boss. I can remember the Saturday morning waltz when some of us worked a 5½ day week. The boss would receive a constant procession of callers anxious to be seen and determined to get in the last word of the week so the boss would have the rest of the weekend to think about it. The office floor was built around a central well so you could do a complete circuit, and at any moment from 11 a.m. to 12.30 p.m. there would be two or three on the prowl, waiting for the moment to get in and see the boss, or thinking up a new excuse to open his door and see who was in there. The boss, fully aware of the position, would sometimes disappear down the back stairs and leave them prowling.

A man likes to know the rules of the game he is playing and he does not like the goal posts to be moved in the middle of the match. He needs to know what to expect from his boss and to ensure that he can succeed as a result. The presence of a colleague with power over your boss which you can be fairly certain is not going to be exercised for your benefit is a threat. When threatened, men respond in one of three ways: they fight it, they sink under or run away from it, or they transfer it to another. A man in the crowd at a football match will transfer the threat posed by relationships at work by abusing authority in the form of the referee. If managers feel the need to transfer the threat in a business, there is trouble.

This departmental pecking order bred just this situation in the 1960s and gave rise to periods of involvement with the behavioural sciences where executives attended managerial Grids, T Groups and seminars on sensitivity. Groups of managers would be sent for a week or so to some secluded hotel where everyone's style of management and behaviour would be analysed. There would develop a fascinated pre-occupation with the effect you had on others and, more importantly, the effect thay had on you. "Good morning" – "What do you mean by that?" This was said to me during a particularly intensive bout of organisational hypochondria which left little time or nervous energy for getting on and running the business.

Some of the experiences were positively damaging to the mental stability of those who took part. Indeed, if you were likely to be unaffected in any negative way by such a shattering experience, the chances were that you did not need to attend in the first place. The T Group is completely unstructured. Some 20 people would assemble with a psychologist who would introduce the session with such words as, "We are here to discover more about ourselves and identify the effect we have on others" and leave it at that. There would then be a pained silence until one group member, trying to break the ice, would suggest that someone should be chairman. He would very likely be told by some of the others that no-one asked him to take the lead, and why was he appointing himself the spokesman in any case?

Over a period of two weeks all the facades would be stripped away and one's true feelings towards the other group members revealed. In effect, a mirror would be held up to each participant by the others, cracks and all. Often the whole underpinning of a man's self-confidence would be kicked away and nothing constructive put in its place.

The Group would then disperse and try to resume their jobs of leading others to objectives, beset by doubts and tormented with feelings of inadequacy. In theory, T Groups were supposed to cleanse the atmosphere between teams of specialists and colleagues and there must have been some successes, but the experience was so dangerous as to be avoided by the majority.

There were experiments where the wives were invited to participate also, and that added a dimension which transcended business and took the joint experience into the home and family to heaven knows what havoc in some households.

The main flood of behavioural scientists, consultants and advisers began to retreat whence it originated – westwards across the Atlantic – as it was realised that the departmental pecking order had serious drawbacks. It gave way to a new sense of direction which was all about pursuing objectives which all understood and with which all could identify. Here, through such aids as management by objectives and key result areas, was and still is the opportunity to look outwards.

An outward looking business is a more healthy one to work in than an inward looking collection of departments fighting for a place in an ever-changing pecking order; for if it is run wisely, all managers and staff will have their share of clear goals. All are to be judged on their performance, and success is clearly seen when it is achieved and clearly seen to be absent if it is not.

The company establishes its profit objective and this becomes the foundation of the work of all its executives, as their share of the total is split out to each department and unit. Each factory manager and sales manager knows what he has to do to enable the company to achieve its objective, and knows also that performance will be judged against that share of the objective.

This sense of purpose and clear objective is clean and straightforward, and managers are also fully visible. It affords no protection to the inept and incompetent, who cannot hide behind confusion and uncertainty. In the last few years new challenges have been thrust onto business, as government involvement and interference has brought forth massive legislation to divert management from its more traditional role. A business has to be even clearer about its goals in these circumstances, as the obstacle course becomes difficult to identify and stick to consistently. Is it the shareholders, the government or the unions whom one is trying to satisfy? Can decisions concerning profitability be made if they mean factory closures and redundancies, or is it inevitable that the State will step in and bolster the uneconomic with government money in return for participation?

One government swings towards intervention and another aims to move away from it, while the problems remain much the same.

All businesses have an atmosphere of their own, even though they may not have identified it. Each will almost certainly fall into one of the categories described above, but may contrive a combination, to the greater or lesser confusion of those who try to determine where the power lies, who makes the decisions and what makes the business tick.

It follows that those who work for any length of time with success must become practitioners in the particular atmosphere, and an awareness of this is of first importance in studying the behaviour and thought processes of your boss. He will be a creature of the environment if he has climbed the ladder in the environment. He will have learned how to adapt to it if he has come to the company from outside. He will know what is applauded, rewarded or frowned upon. Maybe he will be good at demonstrating his ability to act to reinforce this system so his bosses regard him as a loyal company man; safe, reliable and co-operative. Maybe he is quietly overturning it and carrying through a revolution designed to give the business a future with or without the establishment. Your own behaviour in relation to the atmosphere will be an important judgement area of you by your boss, so it is doubly desirable to analyse it. If you have any drive at all you will be trying to change things. The way in which you do it, and the bow wave you set up or avoid, will be one of the keys to your success.

It is all too easy to take on the camouflage of a business and become part of the scenery before you realise it. When you start defending those frustrations you at one time attacked, then is the time to take a look at your cutting edge. All change starts with protest and the transition from protest in its favour to protest against it, is an insidious one which can creep up on you as risk taking comes second to comfort.

The ability, or lack of it, to adapt to the atmosphere is often the deciding factor in a man's career with his company. It is also the major variable when changing jobs. When a man changes his job he will be influenced by the magnet of opportunity or the crowbar prising him loose from the job he is leaving, or both. It is important to his career that he determines correctly which of these influences is stronger, for if he mistakes a refuge from a hostile atmosphere for an opportunity, he will not only be fooling himself, but exchanging one misery for another.

Those who would successfully manage their boss need

first to understand this background against which he operates. So before deciding what makes your boss tick, it is desirable to examine the setting in which he does it.

The easiest pecking order to identify is the one where the proprietor is still active in the business. The most difficult is where the movement of favour from one department to another leads to treacherous shifts of allegiances and political intrigues. One characteristic of this latter atmosphere is the growth of a large central staff to co-ordinate and monitor. This is usually built up to ensure the ascendancy of one function by a strong personality and then matched elsewhere by a rival seeking to correct the balance of power. Staff functions are the obvious candidates for this empire building and monuments to the importance of individuals, whether it is Personnel, Computers, Finance. If allowed, or unable to be stopped, they can take on a dimension quite out of keeping with the normal and sensible central control and discipline which any well run company needs to function efficiently.

The presence of a central personnel function particularly, can cause substantial diversion of nervous energy. It starts with the administration of the Group's personnel manual and grows through salary administration to management development, industrial relations, health and safety, training and organisational development until its ponderous size, interventionist role and quite unrelated time scale sets up a neurosis among operating companies which causes continuing conflict. It is perceived to have substantial power at Head Office – an impression it does nothing to discourage – and the destiny of those who struggle to run the business at the sharp end, on its hands. The penalty for offending any section of this all-pervading spectator is thought to be career damaging, whilst the help it offers when the chips are down is by no means always relevant or forthcoming. If your boss appears to have to check his actions at the centre in a way which delays decisions, stifles initiative or demonstrates a reluctance to manage for fear of rebuke from a central function, then the situation has gone too far. If he is required to comply with some straightforward rules and time scale where the centre needs to be informed or consulted, then the situation is well balanced.

In such circumstances the business will have reached a healthy state of searching after truth and its management will be encouraged to look outwards in pursuit of clear goals. In such an atmosphere figures are designed to reveal the facts rather than conceal them. If you live in an atmosphere of truth you can spend your time making things happen rather than covering up what has happened.

The role of the centre is therefore an important clue to the influences at work in the business, and for the most part the leaner the centre the more opportunity there is for good managers to perform.

Where the relationships between people are concerned, everything flows from the atmosphere in the company. Business is all about relationships between people, and identification of the atmosphere is the first task.

"If the lift failed, he could climb the stairs two at a time . . ."

2. Boss Image and Behaviour

Sitting in your boss's office where he is king, surrounded by his tribal regalia, you are invited to form an impression of his authority. In the same way as the captain of a ship wears a cap with gold braid to denote the symbol of his authority, when a beret would be just as, if not more, comfortable, a manager will have about him some acknowledged symbols which proclaim his authority visually, although they may not be strictly necessary to the performance of his job. Maybe his coffee is brought into his office in a china cup, or on a tray in a pot. He may have one telephone on a six foot desk, or two telephones and an intercom on a side table next to his nine foot desk. He may be entitled to curtains, or mock curtains which can't be drawn, but look like the real thing. Or maybe he has reached a level where he is entitled to real curtains which do pull, but which of course are never closed, to avoid speculation as to why they need to be. Possibly he eats and washes only with his colleagues and superiors, (up to a certain level) or will do so on his next promotion, when he will be invested with the coveted key to the wash room. Whatever he has, it will be more than you have, and you will expect this additional degree of recognition when you get his job.

Businesses vary in their attitude towards status symbols, and some individuals take them more seriously than others. We expect those in authority over us to play the role we assign to them in a way that satisfies our respect for authority. The British Monarchy attracts to itself the trappings of pomp and circumstance, in a way which makes British ceremonial the envy of the world, and a source of pride to Britain. The Catholic church displays colour and riches in the poorest parts of the world, and has a greater grip on the imagination of its followers than many other religions. Factory workers expect to see their chairman's wife wearing a mink coat when she attends a social function.

When Lady Docker was the wife of the chairman of BSA she gave a new dimension to the concept of ostentation. Her exhibitionism included a gold plated Daimler, gold lame clothes and very expensive mink – even the seats of her special motor car were covered with it: perhaps the pleasure of resting the elegantly clad posterior on such opulence made up for the heat such contact must have generated. There was much comment at the time from the press and the City, but the work force at BSA were generally enthusiastic. The boss and his lady must be on a pedestal, for that, after all, keeps alive the hope that one day you might occupy the dizzy heights yourself. Furthermore, we like to look up to those set above us as a reassurance that we are working in a structure of substance. What respect can we command from the world when those several layers above us go around looking humble and as if they have not two coins to rub together? The boss who indulges himself in democratic humility or self denial may be setting an example to those who tend to be unnecessarily extravagant, and at times all organisations need such an example, but in the long run the layers of the hierarchy need the plumage which is accorded them by those of lesser plumage who have ambition and a need for recognition. If you wish to recruit high calibre people from outside, you will find it much more difficult if your company is seen to be frugal and lacking in style. Recognition as the main motivator demands a standard of external recognition that is a shorthand for explaining what you are.

Your boss has a need to present you with an image of authority, which he will find easier to do when he is the senior man present than when his own seniors are around. It is very interesting to observe how the boss's behaviour changes when his boss confronts him in your presence. Perhaps he is laying down the law in his office, giving you his views with force and vigour, or playing god, when the phone rings, and his boss is at the other end of the line doing the same thing. You then witness the sort of pressures your boss has to deal with, and if he has a rough ride in your presence it is difficult for him to recapture the atmosphere that existed before his phone call. It is essential to your understanding of your boss to see him in different degrees of tension with his boss, and those to whom he must relate.

At one time I worked for a man, whom let us call Adolf. He had an outsized ego to make up for a diminutive stature. He could be moved to a state of near apoplexy if thwarted and give an outward impression of authority with a will that was not to be trifled with. On each Monday afternoon, we both used to attend a meeting with his boss and his and my colleagues, and because of Adolf's long service and status, he always occupied the arm chair adjacent to the Big Boss's desk, *facing* the rest of the meeting. This, in itself, was regarded as a symbol of recognition, but the crowning example to us all of the level to which Adolf had risen, was when Big Boss took a box of Havana cigars from his desk, helped himself and then offered it to Adolf – in that order. Adolf's eyes would rest on the drawer from the start of the meeting, and would relax when the ceremony was completed – usually ten minutes after the meeting got under way. With his cigar alight he would settle contentedly, yet malevolently, into his armchair, well established on the judgement bench and gloat at the rest of us puffing on cheroots or cigarettes which came with saving stamps. One Monday, Big Boss had given up smoking and forgot, or determined not to offer Adolf a cigar. The effect was disturbing. Adolf fidgeted, his eyes fixed on the drawer for most of the meeting, making little or no contribution, and the rest of us watched fascinated as the ultimate status symbol continued to be withheld. Adolf interpreted this as a fall from grace, and for several days was miserably deflated, regaining his composure and bombast only when the ritual was resumed the following week.

Power does peculiar things to bosses. Some adorn themselves with a physical helplessness which is completely bogus, for they would never have climbed to their position if they really could not do without a chauffeur, who not only drives the car but does the shopping, or at least takes the boss's wife shopping, carries the briefcase, adjusts the travelling rug, helps the boss in and out of the car and into the lift. Also a secretary who handles personal mail, prepares cheques for signature and handles the social diary. If this dependence upon an entourage stretches to a personal assistant, remoteness becomes inevitable. This may be a defence mechanism of the busy boss, to keep at bay those whose demands he would rather discourage, but it can also denote the searching for an image which will satisfactorily demonstrate the importance of the position he considers he holds.

I once had a colleague whose first reaction on being promoted was to come into the office thirty minutes later than his hitherto lifelong habit. He could, it seemed, from then on only obtain anyone else on the telephone through his secretary and it took a 15-second delay while the other end held on waiting for him to find it convenient to come on the line. My reaction was to hang up and wait for him to come through direct. His secretary would say that we were cut off, and I used to assure her that I had hung up. This sort of charade did not survive the colleague pressure for very long and got this colleague off to an indifferent start.

Another unfortunate way of drawing attention to your importance is to take telephone calls when juniors are present, and treat them to a lengthy, irrelevant wait whilst you give a demonstration of your interpretation of power in action. If you have ever been subjected to this type of performance, you will know how unimpressive it is, unless of course you are involved in the subject. I usually offer to go and get on with some work and return when the telephone call is over, and this has the effect of shortening it. The assumption that your subordinates' or colleagues' time is less valuable than your own is not only bad manners but counter-productive, for how can they believe you want them to work at pressure, if you merely leave them dangling as bored spectators of your own ego when you meet. Boss imitation is inevitable, so it is as well to show only what you want imitated.

It is interesting to observe, nonetheless, the relationship between what the boss says on the telephone, and the way he relays what he imagines he said later. He might forget you heard the conversation. Indeed he might have meant what he imagines he said, but it did not sound like that at all in the half of the conversation you heard. Transmission is no guarantee of reception. But post-event imagination is no guarantee there has been transmission either.

One is reluctant to deny one's boss this element of fantasy. After all, there can be few of us who do not indulge in it to some extent, and providing we are straight in our dealings and objectives, it takes on a quality which makes us and even our bosses reassuringly human. The public performance of the boss will be different from his face to face style with you. It is well to remember that the individuals who make up the meeting of subordinates are the same as those with whom you have to work individually, and any behaviour when they are all together, which is markedly different from what you would normally display when face to face will be inclined to confuse these relationships. Your subordinates will make some allowance for the pressures of the occasion, but will not accept a level of treatment in the safety of an audience, that you would be disinclined to apply one to one. Your boss has a similar constraint and any apparent unfairness or cheap point scoring at your expense in front of an audience should not be allowed to pass without some sanction at a time of your choosing. There is a fine line between the convention of boss behaviour that the system accepts, and the misuse of power in the safety of numbers. The Chairman can quite reasonably use a gavel at a meeting, although many never find the need, whereas it would be distinctly out of place at a one to one session. The queen bee secretary who filters the outside world from the boss would be less inclined to try the technique on a direct subordinate.

It is interesting to see the boss by chance on holiday, or meet him at some unexpected informal occasion. One boss I worked for used to behave with a well ordered dignity. I saw him one day, whilst we were both on holiday, (separately) and he and his large family were between camping sites. His car, laden with every aid, looked like part of the stage set for the Grapes of Wrath, and he seemed to be about to resume a round the world voyage after being marooned without water for 10 days.

My father-in-law was a distinguished Member of Parliament and used to take part in the annual water sports at a seaside village. He had just emerged from the water after falling from the greasy pole, clad in a set of oilskins, when one of his constituents came and introduced herself and a party of Americans who wanted to study the political system as part of their trip to Europe.

One man I worked for used to give the impression of being a frail but mentally alert vulture. He could just about negotiate the journey from the back seat of his car to the lift in the office block, which would take him to his eyrie on the top floor. All this with the aid of his chauffeur and greeted by his faithful secretary. It was a daily ceremony staged for those who liked majesty in action. If the lift failed he could climb the stairs two at a time. In the office he had a lectern on his desk to hold his open diary. To those sitting on the opposite side of the desk, this book would take on the dimensions of at least some source of religious reference, if not the very tablet itself. In fact it had very little written in it to disturb the social routine of bridge and visits to Specialists. Each year there would be The Progress To The Conference which would add a new impetus to the stories of eccentric behaviour for 12 months to come.

He would always change his hotel suite on arrival on some pretext. We used to warn the hotel manager, because we did not often return to the same place, and he would show Vulture to the secondary suite first, and then to the one booked for his use when he demanded the change. One year he demanded seats in row B for the Edinburgh Festival Tattoo, and not only insisted on this row, but on the seat numbers within it. The whole event was of course, fully booked but that was of no consequence. After prolonged enquiries and negotiations, I had to tell him that it was impossible. We were then treated to the predictable demonstration, and when permitted to speak, I explained that it could be done if he would like to sit with his wife between the trombones and the kettle drums as the first three rows had been removed for the band.

His charismatic personality and sharp mind allowed him to get away with the most extraordinary self indulgence. He also had an unnerving squint which he used to devastating confusion at meetings and conferences. He would point a gnarled finger at one, and look at another, and two voices would speak in unison. At The Conference he would chair the proceedings flanked by a top table from Head Office that extended in a series of dog legs to and along part of the very perimeter of the Conference Hall. Indeed, the cast was at times nearly as big as the audience, although few on the platform contributed more than their august presence.

He would allow the agenda to proceed for about an hour, by which time the awe of the occasion was beginning to wear off the audience. His interventions up to that time would be sparse. Then he would rise whilst the manager conducting the session was in full flight, and tell him to sit down. He would deliver a magisterial rebuke to the Conference for keeping him sitting for a whole hour without a single constructive suggestion being made, and then he would demand that one delegate selected at random, should stand up and tell us all what we ought to do about gaining new dealers whose early closing day differed from the rest of the town. Usually, the more senior you were, the nearer to the front you sat, so familiar faces were near at hand, and new recruits sheltered in relief and boredom at the back. I changed it all around at my first Conference and put the newest in the front.

"You – stand up"
"Me Sir?"
"Me Sir?"
"No not you – you. What have you got to say for yourself?"
"Er well um er"
"What was that?"
"Mumble mumble"
"You should be ashamed of yourself – how long have you been with us?"
"Three days Sir"

One is reluctant to deny a top boss his relaxation on the

golf course, over long lunches, or in whatever way he gets his pleasure. The wear and tear on the physical and nervous systems of being at the top of a business is enormous. Bad news followed by worse news, and an anxious and curious audience waiting for your decisions, studying your reactions, can be uncomfortable, particularly when you have just announced plans based on the situation before the bad news.

There are so many influences beyond one's control – interest rates, rates of exchange, economic climate, commodity prices, government involvement. These can have a traumatic effect on your business overnight. It is not surprising therefore that bosses get snappy, overly assertive or inconsistent. There are days when everything seems to go wrong, and to add to it your subordinates perform with maddening predictability. You wearily accept that having adjusted your own thinking this morning – was it really only this morning? – to a new set of circumstances, the job of adjusting the thinking of your subordinates has yet to be done. Or, worse still, you have to convince your own boss of your new viewpoint, having just got him to understand and accept the one you are now abandoning.

These pressures are constant in any business, and we have to live with them as indeed we have to adjust to the business atmosphere. Often I have wondered how the boss's boss can swallow some of the things I have heard a boss of mine say to him in my presence. How can a man who represents authority two up the line, possibly be gullible enough to believe or even accept, some of the things that are said to him? Maybe he does not accept them and is summing up the boss more shrewdly than I know, which is reassuring. Alternatively, maybe the Big Boss is not such a great man as we had assumed, which while it is disillusioning, adds confidence to promotion prospects, assuming he is good enough to hold the business together until one's time is come.

The higher you climb up the ladder, the less fantasy you are inclined to weave around the men at the top of the business. Closer proximity and more frequent contact strip the mystery from the man who hitherto was a lofty image, pulling the strings with a certainty of touch. Instead, you find a manager who has faced the same sort of problems which you now face, and has either overcome them and brought success, or persuaded his boss that he has overcome them, and concentrated on merchandising his performance to the temporary benefit of his career. If he is a genuinely sound and successful man he has probably succeeded through a combination of ability and doing what others can do but have not done.

Observe your boss in action with his superiors; whether it arouses your admiration or urges you to grind your teeth to powder, you should wonder what is so special about this man who is set in authority over you. He will usually have the ability to project himself, and to generate the impression of effectiveness. Maybe he is effective and just plain competent at his job, and maybe he is a scheming self interested politician who knows how to work the system.

I have known so many people in business, who seemingly go through life achieving precious little. Their subordinates and colleagues know they are ineffective, and yet they prove their capacity for survival time and again, through each reorganisation and change at the top. On the basis that a successful career is a combination of job effectiveness and ability to project and protect yourself, they lean heavily towards skill in the latter. It is doubtless unfair that those men and women get on better who have skill in projection although little job effectiveness, than do those who are good at their jobs but hopeless at projecting themselves. There *is* justice in that most useless, self-projecting people get exposed eventually. The real opportunity is for effective people to start projecting themselves and creating the environment where they can be more successful; then their careers are assured. In a healthy organisation, competent performance brings its own reward.

Boss management is all about the actions that thrusting, self confident people must take in order to win the freedom to perform and thus fulfil themselves. This emphasis is quite different from defensive, sycophantic, ingratiating crawling, that is undertaken out of insecurity and as a cover for inadequacy. Let the creeps pussyfoot around their bosses if they get any satisfaction from it. You should strive to win your independence and develop a mutual respect, which will either take you upwards at your boss's instigation, or take you upwards at your own. The ideal situation is where both you and your boss acknowledge that you are both good operators and are jointly pursuing a career plan for you, to which you are both committed. This spirit of partnership brings with it a large measure of job satisfaction. For there is mutual trust, and an all out effort on the part of both of you, to expand the business and promote your career to which it is linked. It will not do your boss any harm either, to have achieved results through you and to have provided the business with an effective thruster ready for further promotion.

You owe yourself the determination to use what you have without limitation. This includes influencing, if not controlling, what becomes of you in this once only appearance, (we think) on this planet, for a few short years in the scale of human evolution.

It is your life. It belongs to you and to no one else. It certainly does not belong to your boss. The main reason for failure in this life stems from the inability or unwillingness to use all one has without limitation. We need goals and the complete belief that we can attain them with the thrust to overcome inertia. It is a matter of attitude.

3. What Makes the Boss Tick?

Your boss is a central figure in your life, and if you are to succeed in living in harmony with him you will want to understand what makes him tick. Every conscious action he takes will have a motive behind it, and the first stage is to consider what it might be.

The main motivators are reckoned to be;

Recognition
Reward
Romance
Immortality.

All of us are driven by one or more of these four, and the man or woman for whom you work is no exception.

Recognition

Depending on whether he is confident or insecure, ambitious or content, so your boss's desire for recognition will be designed to secure his promotion, maintain his position, develop or secure his reputation.

An insecure boss is the most difficult to work for as his fears make rational discussion and decision making random and unpredictable. In all his dealings with others, the spectre of his own boss or some other influence such as creditors or shareholders, will be present, questioning and challenging. You need to be able to feel the presence of this third party, and to acknowledge that the man you work for is motivated by a desire or need to satisfy it, and thus obtain recognition for doing so. Such a situation makes relationships difficult if you too are insecure, or do not have such an understanding. For if your boss is an instrument of the man above, and you do not know what to do to satisfy either of them on any consistent basis, you cannot obtain recognition for yourself, and one of your own key motivations is unfulfilled.

The key is in helping your boss to satisfy his boss and in time the use of this technique can be just as effective when you withhold your help, as when you give it. Your boss comes to rely on you, quite rightly, and you are able to forge a spirit of partnership with him in the task of satisfying those who make demands upon him.

There are some clear symptoms of insecurity. If you ask your boss a question, does he hedge and procrastinate and then some hours or days later come back to you with a positive or negative response, in words that are obviously not his? Does he shift his ground after pressure from above, or from his colleagues or subordinates? Does he refer you to another for a decision which he will accept as binding on himself? Maybe he leaves you with the sticky problems and identifies himself with successes. Perhaps he gets bad tempered and shouts when cornered for a decision.

I had an insecure boss who would always stand up and walk around the room when called upon to make a decision. He would glance hopefully at the door imploring an interruption. If help failed to arrive he would hunt among his papers for an urgent memo he had just remembered to deal with. Then he would put it down and ask who else you had discussed the matter with. He would be very helpful in nominating others as potential sounding boards for the idea. In the end you either made the decision yourself, or it got lost in the endless round of getting other people's views. In such a system the timid never did anything, and the bold got away with murder.

Where the insecure man is, in some ways the hardest to work for, he is the easiest to manage from below, for he is vulnerable and dependent on ingratiating himself with his boss. The secure and confident boss may not be as secure and confident as he seems. He has his problems, but he puts a different face on them to show those around him that he is on top of the job. His motivation will be the recognition of his effectiveness and efficiency. This requires the support of those who work for him. You can best handle him by letting him see that you respond most effectively when helped and encouraged, and in these circumstances you are productive and creative. When pushed around or made to look small in the presence of others, however, your work and response to his needs will never be as creative as when encouraged. He may be inclined to show off in public and use his power and the occasion to cause discomfort.

A good sign of security in a boss is his willingness to take decisions and positive action on his own initiative. He will do so whether invited to or not. What you therefore need to watch is that you do not give him unwelcome openings to come into your area and make decisions that you should be making. If you do not take action, he will. It is well to determine early on, therefore, the degree to which your boss is secure or insecure.

Recognition or lack of it must come from above, from below or from equals, and it helps to work out from where your boss seeks his. Maybe he wants to be seen as a strong man by you and your colleagues, more than he wants to be seen as a good colleague by his peers. Or does he want to be the efficient instrument of his boss? He will be subject to pressure from some source, and your skill is to assess where this is.

If he seeks it from his own boss, the situation is fairly straightforward. If he seeks it from one or more of his colleagues it is more complex. Perhaps one of those colleagues is difficult to get on with, protective of his own area and critical of everyone else's. Yet this colleague may have considerable influence with the boss which your boss shares with him. This has the makings of a political atmosphere which if it cannot be avoided, has to be lived with until it can be changed. Your boss will feel he needs to keep in with this powerful colleague, and will be influenced by his giving or withholding approval. So in your dealings with the boss you will want to be aware of this consideration, or possibly this preoccupation.

Supposing your boss runs sales, and this powerful colleague runs production, the normal push and shove between the two will take on a new dimension if production has more influence, interest and attention from your boss's boss. You will be encouraged to avoid making waves, and to live with this situation rather than fight it. Such a prostitution of freedom of action and integrity is to be deplored, and any executive with spirit will seek the opportunity to redress the balance. This will surely come as the favoured department drops a clanger, which is the chance to get the relationship onto a more even footing.

You can be sure that recognition is the motivating factor behind the awkward colleague too and his aggressive attention seeking is directed to this end. If you can ensure that the recognition also applies to inept performance, then the balance tips to equilibrium, and you do a service to your boss in the process. I can recall such an experience when the production manager was inclined to be self centred, self proclaiming, clever yet badly integrated. He had everyone jumping, and a substantial influence over our joint boss, which was perhaps more imagined than real, but was nevertheless dangerous for those into whom he had sunk his knife this month. We had a major product launch planned to follow the commissioning of a new plant installed at his instigation, and at vast cost. The launch meeting to the sales force and then to the trade was all fixed, and the campaign under starter's orders. But when it came to the date, he had still not commissioned his plant and we had to cancel the launch. He agreed to attend the meeting where this would be done and explain why he had let us down. To his credit he did this with clarity and integrity. From then on the balance was more even, while he tried to gain the recognition I told him we would be prepared to give if he could fulfil our expectations of him – which tended to increase all the time.

Sideways pressures are part of the cut and thrust of business, and gamesmanship is to be expected at times. But a weak colleague tends to get squeezed by those who are more skilled and ruthless at pushing their departments.

If a boss seeks constant approval from below, he will

be unlikely to last long. Subordinates will jostle each other for the power to exert the greatest influence and leverage on him, in the knowledge that he is not strong enough to prevent it. The power struggle will cause constantly changing pressures among colleagues, and as the axes are ground, gangs will form around and against the strongest influence. If this is you, then you will spend more time watching your back than doing your job, and if it is not, then you will be equally diverted. In these circumstances, the team will never be happy and the boss will fail in his objectives. The effect this has up the line will probably cause him to be removed and replaced by someone more decisive and effective.

This sort of uncertainty can originate from weakness, which makes you wonder how he came to be there at all, or it can be as a result of a shattering experience described earlier, to exposure to some form of sensitivity training where the effect he has had upon others has been analysed to the point of gibbering ambivalence. I have seen a boss bounced around like a pea on a drum by a group of subordinates, each trying to advance his point of view, and the boss incapable of deciding anything because his objectives were not clear, and his managerial style distorted. All that was needed was a decisive statement after rational discussion and the team would have closed ranks and responded. A quest to be popular and avoid upsetting anyone usually results in lack of decision, and then such decisions as are taken are altered as soon as one colleague expresses his opposition or disappointment. There is no substitute for a firm hand on the helm in pursuit of a commonly held objective, to cut the cackle and achieve results which in themselves bring the long term recognition.

One might imagine that an example of a secure boss is the up and coming family member who is destined to inherit the crown, and who has sufficient private means to be spared the worry of being out of work if he fails to perform. Some of the most anxious people, however, fall into this category, for they strive continually to be recognised as competent executives in their own right. From an early age they will have had a sense of destiny and inheritance drummed into them, and in all their contacts, in and with the business, there will be a sense of progressive movement, stopping for a while here and there but always getting nearer to an inevitable destination. If this facility is made available to, and taken up by young family members who would be quite unable to succeed elsewhere, then how difficult it is for a member of the family who is of average competence or better, to be taken seriously and evaluated not for who he is, but for what he is.

It is difficult to relate to non-family when your every word and action is weighed against the certain belief that you will go to the top regardless. To be seen as something special gives one a distorted view of oneself and encourages behaviour which would not survive the first brawl or mauling in the real world. Arrogance is excused if not expected. Demands on subservient people can be made without justification or explanation, and service to personal needs and whims can transcend the normal means of gaining the willing co-operation of others.

The pressures are just as strong when the traditions of the family lean exceptionally in the other direction. Where extreme kindness, consideration and encouragement of people, rather than performance is the order of things, the young family member can feel intolerance and frustration at the seeming unawareness of his uncles and cousins that the world outside has changed.

Ownership, if anything, enhances the tensions, because unless you sell out, and with it cast away the enduring source of the family fortune, to the howls of the widows and aunts and retired directors and relations, you are on a treadmill only an owner can understand. The relentless pressure grinds on without relief.

Working for a member of the family has its compensations. It places a convenient limitation on what you have to do to obtain respectable recognition. You will not be expected to go any higher, because only the family does that. Once you have made the level which non-family man aspires to, you can relax and look forward to maintaining this gracious state until your name is called for a gold watch and a retirement speech. The peace can be badly shattered when a fan light in the ceiling opens and a non-family man climbs through, to be followed by others brought in from outside.

Suddenly you have to explain why it is not you occupying these new heights. You have to be prepared to be responsible to a non-family member, whose judgement of you is likely to be based on achievement to come, rather than on services rendered. If this is tough for you, then it is just as tough for those who are sharing or relinquishing power for the first time. New standards of performance and ways of doing things, new perspectives on the erstwhile courtiers who accepted that the family ran the business in all its components, puts new pressures on the relationships.

When security founded on an established pecking order in the protective atmosphere of a family business, gives way to a more demanding and open ended judgement, where nothing is inevitable any more, new values are needed to avoid distracting insecurity. If performance becomes the key to security, then objectives and help are needed to obtain performance.

The boss who is most inclined to be secure is the one who can turn in the results. He is the one who can fulfil the expectations of those he must satisfy, whether financial institutions, shareholders, Board or boss. He knows his reputation will spread beyond the confines of his present company – it probably has already – which could be why he works where he does. If for some reason he falls out with his boss, he will be snapped up by others who want his services. Such performance brings with it a new pride in the team he leads, and the values applied in this atmosphere provide a real alternative to paternal and protective security.

Recognition has as much to do with reputation as it has with reward. The systematic build up of a sound name for good performance and effectiveness in each job tackled, is something which no material reward can give or buy. There are those who seek recognition at the expense of material reward, and who will experience a greater degree of fulfilment from the applause or top billing, than the pay cheque which accompanies the work. Some people will do anything for publicity, or to get talked about, or perhaps to be recognised in the street; to receive the homage of those you yourself respect is one of the leading motivations in life. To be seen in the company of the exalted, or to be seen to be recognised and acknowledged by the famous, will take the place of much silent material payment which is subject to tax deduction. To receive a letter of thanks for work done from the boss, or in a voluntary organisation from a respected figure, is worth more than a sum of money could secure. It is worth living a hundred years to receive a telegram from the Sovereign. To wear the chain of office as first citizen and pay out of your own pocket for the privilege, is considered worthwhile by those who do it. The 'honour' is the rationale for it, when 'recognition' would probably be a more accurate description.

Reward

It is not a simple matter to separate reward from recognition because these two motivations are closely entwined. Money is the most practical and popular reward for one's efforts, because it can be used to show the world to what degree you have been recognised. It can feed the ego-need to endow a hospital, or it can buy an impressive holiday, a good address, education for your children, clothes for your wife, or a sports car.

However, reward goes much deeper than money. In a business, the reward for success can be the satisfaction of achievement, freedom to come and go without having to ask permission or be checked up on. Freedom to incur expenses with periodic rather than immediate scrutiny because you are trusted, as a reward for what you have accomplished and are expected to accomplish. A good boss will get great satisfaction and reward from gathering around himself successful people whom he can develop for promotion. He will feel a sense of real commitment towards you if he has fledged you and you are making good in his or another department.

He may feel it is reward enough to know he has his own boss's confidence, and he can trust that his salary and future will be nurtured by a grateful boss, so he can get on and do his job without continuing anxiety. From your point of view, you should endeavour to analyse what he considers important as reward. To do this, there is no substitute for discussing it at an appropriate time. He is probably lonely, and needs to be able to talk about himself. One of his rewards may be to find you a sympathetic listener to his problems. If you want to find out what makes your boss tick, you can do worse than create the atmosphere in which he wants to tell you.

The monetary reward has to be adequate for the job done and the risk taken. If it is not, and too much reliance placed on non-material rewards which border closely on recognition, businesses are inclined to develop workforces which are understretched, overstaffed, ageing and unlikely to find a job elsewhere at the same level.

If the risk of the work, and the atmosphere of the firm, is such that the recognition and reward go hand in hand with high salary if you perform, and the sack if you do not, then the values of the team will be geared to rapacious pursuit of salary and selling out to the highest bidder when the heat comes on. Such companies have an antiseptic, authoritarian feel about them and some are highly successful. Part of the recognition of those who have been exposed to such an atmosphere might be that they have endured it and can offer the experience to the next employer, as part of a pedigree leading to a goal in company number four in five years' time. So recognition comes later. In the meantime the reward has to compensate, and that had better be good and stay good.

Romance

For examples of romance as a driving force you need look no further than the ardent lover and his lass. The lengths to which some will go to get the boy or girl of their dreams transcends hardship, cost, position and opportunity while the chase is on. Once completed it can be another matter. The pursuit rather than the kill is the thrill of the hunt. There are those who pursue romantic dreams all their lives and get satisfaction from imagining they have found their Valhalla. How else do we explain those who opt for the simple life and get their satisfaction from a cottage in a peat bog with no modern amenities, no pressure, no money and no material rewards? No recognition after the first envious words of encouragement from ex-colleagues at the farewell party, who continue to commute and strive for recognition and reward via the 8.15 each day.

The pursuit of dreams and fantasies, excitement and romance is a thread which runs through us all to some extent. From an advanced case such as Don Quixote or Walter Mitty, to the average cinema audience transported for 1½ hours to some imagery well outside the confines of commuter land, the No 8 bus or luncheon vouchers, romance plays a part in our lives and adds impetus to the hard graft and daily grind. We might win a lottery and if we did we would buy a villa in Spain, a boat, brown ale with every meal, or champagne for breakfast and a joint of beef each Sunday.

"I'd pick you up on a Persian carpet, my dear, and whisk you away to Arabia and we'd live in the desert under the stars until we decided to do something else – but right now I must put the cat out". We should not underestimate the dreamers. They provide a dimension in business which most of us are too busy to dwell upon, and sometimes come up with ideas of a relevance and simplicity which stop the practical hard workers in their tracks.

Success will buy the opportunity for romance for the young man just setting out and is a strong motivator while the dream is fresh. As time goes on, when it does not pay the gas bill or the shareholders' dividends, romance is inclined to take a lower place in our motivation, but it will break out from time to time, or become the fallback to which we revert when the realities of more practical objectives fall short of expectancy. To throw it all over and seek some self fulfilment at the end of the rainbow is an emotional option which takes courage, desperation or irresponsibility, but it is there below the surface.

Women may seem to have a more developed romantic sense than men but in many ways they are more practical. As the man talks about getting away from it all and living a self sufficient dream, the woman will want to know how far away she will be from mother, or how near to the shops. But she will remember anniversaries, like having her hand held, keep up the yearly traditions and read the old bedtime stories to the children. She'll get her lift from a hairdo, make-up, new clothes and home improvement, and this will be only partially to satisfy her desire to impress the girl friends and neighbours. She'll read romantic stories in women's magazines and lap them up as an antidote to the daily chores. She will serve a Christmas pudding at the end of Christmas lunch, but not because she believes her family lacks nourishment at that stage in the meal.

Romance can provide the drive to keep two homes going, with the man playing the head of the family role in one and Don Juan in the other. The company car can be the trusty steed of the gun slinging adventurer, the armoured vehicle which takes you into battle, or a jet fighter. The passage in the office block can be the stage set for High Noon or the run up to a cricket pitch or the aisle of a cathedral, and the entry to the car park can be the sweep into the parade ground. If you think this is far-fetched ask any psychologist why fins were put on the back of motor cars as seemingly useless pieces of styling. Why has the shape of the Coca Cola bottle been so successful? We cannot live without hope, which tends more or less to fantasy according to the individual's need to cope with the daily grind.

Immortality

When an ageing professional who has made as much money as he or she can spend in the years remaining, and gained fame and prestige in the process, does not know when to quit, the chances are you are seeing a bid for immortality. It happens to politicians, actors, boxers, businessmen whose remaining ambition after a career of success is to become a legend, or at least secure a place in history. There is no doubt immortality is a motivator when you look at the statues of long forgotten worthies providing a perch for the pigeons or a stopping place for dogs. Consider the effort and drive which must have gone into the decision to erect the statue. Maybe the individual provided the money for it himself or made his family's inheritance conditional upon its erection.

From the Board Room portrait to the endowment of a

building, from the provision for a scholarship to the setting up of a monument, the urge to be remembered, to live on beyond the short time allowed us, has been a major drive through all history. It is closely tied in with the ego and self fulfilment layers of the hierarchy of human needs, which is described later, and represents one of the great sources of drive and enterprise of which innovation and service to fellow human beings is made. For to be remembered by others implies that you have done something either for them or to them. The former is more likely to yield an affectionate memorial than the latter. But such is life that it is often the dictators who get the graven images.

Millions of Buddhists believe this life is only one stage in the journey to enlightenment, and one's conduct during this span will determine one's position in the next. To millions of others who hold no such beliefs, the thought of returning to nothingness at death is abhorrent and gives impetus to the belief in a Supreme Being who has a purpose in the creation of life and a plan for the physically dead at the end of it. Do we really get born again, or live on and meet our loved ones and erstwhile earthly acquaintances when we die? Maybe. If so, do we behave, achieve and perform on earth in a manner consistent with that prospect?

The Christian ethic, or other religious code of behaviour which accepts a concern for others and a set of civilised values for oneself, lies behind much of what we do on this earth. At times we wonder perhaps if the boss has heard of it or knows what he is in for in another place. Is he after fame or notoriety – does he want a monument or an epitaph?.

He has a lonely job.

The higher he rises in the organisation, the lonelier it becomes, for three reasons;

(a) The pyramid narrows and there are fewer colleagues in close proximity.

(b) He may develop a belief that it is undignified to fraternise with his subordinates.

(c) Subordinates are wary of being seen too much in his company in case they are believed by their colleagues to be crawling.

From your point of view, this third aspect is one of the key hurdles to overcome if you are to work closely with your boss. Much of the tension between boss and subordinate is caused by the unwillingness to cross this line to friendship for fear of developing familiarity, in case both lose some independence. Play acting, point scoring and posing then get in the way of a desirable relationship. He needs to feel respected, if not actually loved. He has no way of telling for certain what those below think of him. If you only tell him you think he is wonderful, he will either be suspicious or inflated, and become impossible. If you merely argue and disagree and are difficult, he will feel the need to assert his authority before the criticism gets out of hand. He will remember you as unhelpful when he has the option to help you at a later date. You need to be able to talk frankly with him and put yourself in the position where he values your views because they are candid, unfearing and valid. He will be more wary of putting on a great ego-act for your benefit when he knows it will cut little ice, and perhaps prove his need to cover some weakness or anxiety.

He likes to know the effect he is having on those around him and if you can show him you are the barometer of feeling which he must consult frequently, you will have achieved a good rapport with him. It is devastating for a boss to see a bleak, disapproving reception on the face of a respected subordinate after a tirade or an irrational outburst. He will appreciate the look of genuine enthusiasm and approval for a piece of rapport that will lead to wholehearted implementation and follow through. In the process of boss management, one part consists of withholding approval and the other of giving it wholeheartedly. You should carry out well, quickly and willingly that to which you are committed, while what you do not approve will need to be thrashed out until you agree with it or agree to differ, and then either do it or go. The boss will be quick to appreciate that to get things done through and by you, whom he trusts and respects, you work very much better when he takes you along with him. It is always better to come up with a positive alternative suggestion for those edicts with which you do not agree. In this way you continue to be positive, helpful and productive, which is after all the way to succeed. It also flushes out the irrational or political decisions, so that at least you know what is bugging the boss, and maybe your idea will get you both off the hook.

4. The Rabbit Garden

If you have a productive vegetable garden full of the fruits of your labour, towards which you have a feeling of ownership and pride, you will try hard to keep the rabbits out.

There are three ways to do this:

1. Exterminate the rabbits. This is usually not practical and your garden will go to seed while you spend time chasing them.
2. Build a fence to keep them out. This is expensive and has to be very deep to prevent them burrowing underneath, and strong to stop them gnawing through it. It also has to be well maintained.
3. Plant a rabbit garden around your vegetable garden. That is you plant some interesting food deliberately between the rabbits and your garden so they never get beyond this strip and leave the rest alone.

You have much the same sort of alternatives with your boss, and the third option is by far the most effective not to say practical.

The freedom which comes from effective boss management starts with the achievement of room to manoeuvre and to run your affairs with the minimum of interference. This presupposes that you use this freedom to do what you and the boss have agreed needs doing; that objectives are achieved and the boss has a true, regular and accurate feedback about what is going on. Freedom to act should not in any circumstances include freedom to hoodwink the boss. You have no right whatever to do so. The company pays your salary and you are a responsible member who is entrusted with part of it. In no way does title pass to you when you take responsibility for a job. You are however, entitled to be allowed to get on with what you have been given to do without a lot of unhelpful heavy breathing down your neck, and without the boss continually pulling up the plant to see if it is growing. In this you are entitled to defend yourself against interference and distraction.

What you put in the rabbit garden will depend upon the mentality of your boss. Does he like to pick up the twigs while you are trying to move the trees? If so put up items for his attention which will satisfy this need. The layout of a brochure, the design of a menu for a presentation dinner, details of a press release, his advice on the colour for a particular pack design. You then have freedom to move. He will require his regular figures about the performance of the business, but he will leave you alone to organise, and run your affairs to a greater extent if you go out of your way to involve him in part of them, than if you try to exclude him from all of them, or try to ignore him. You should never try to ignore or underestimate your boss. You may see in him characteristics that make him far from perfect in your eyes, but he will have a basic need to assert his authority. This may be quiet and long in coming but it will come. Whatever he is like he is entitled to the courtesy of your attention, and to your acceptance that he is the boss, whatever the justice, good fortune or inexplicable act of fate that put him in that position. You have no justification in treating him with discourtesy or with condescension. You may not want to wake him up or even bring him back to life. You certainly do not want to anger him into giving you a convincing demonstration that he is the boss.

No doubt you have observed how he is programmed to react in a predictable way to given situations or information. Your aim is to avoid those reactions which are unhelpful or intrusive, but to encourage those which keep his attention on the plants in the rabbit garden.

If you are skilful in controlling the items to which the boss gives his attention, you can work to make him helpful and supportive. It is important to avoid a situation where he is unpredictable and likely to descend on an area which will distract you and do little to advance your progress to objectives. Worse still, it may cause confusion with your team if sudden new and urgent demands are made when their programmes are already committed. The key ingredient in this process of restricting the boss's involvement is to produce results. If your results are poor, or worse still, are different from those you have predicted and discussed in advance with him, then you must expect some trampling on your prize plants in the course of an investigation to establish just what is going on that he does not know about. It is good management and bears the hallmarks of integrity to avoid surprises. If you are going off track, tell him – never hope that it will get better and he will not find out. What's the secret anyway? If you are well on track, tell him and excite him. You need a skilful balance of competent management yielding results, good communication of those results for better or worse, forecast consistent with practice and a shrewdly sown rabbit garden to absorb his interest in areas where he can help and keep him away from areas where he could cause confusion if not chaos.

It may be you will misjudge the amount you put in the rabbit garden. If you start off with too little you will be subjected to much questioning and cross-examination – that is a bad position from which to try to manage your boss. The way to correct this situation is to go to the other extreme and take a lot of information to him for discussion. You need to make it clear that you can and will, if permitted, deal with all such matters yourself, but as the boss is clearly so interested in all aspects of your affairs, you feel he will wish to be involved. This will not last long and then you can settle into a more selective rabbit garden.

If your boss is an irritating nit picker, one helpful way of speeding up the process is to ensure that you seek his help on a wide range of trivial matters at meetings which you arrange just before lunch or at 5 p.m. – preferably on Fridays. Also, it can help, when you make the agenda for your boss, (which you should always do) you put the trivia first. In this way there will never be time to discuss the more important areas of boss involvement and he will soon want to be selective. The skill is in this selection. Maybe to you it is trivia, but to him it is a legitimate area of involvement. If he is any good as a boss he will have some creative ideas which you will not have thought of. Some of those will be worth pursuing and you should do so wholeheartedly. If you have a closed mind to his suggestions you are asking for him to find a way in, as well as missing out on ideas which could be good for the business.

I once had a boss whose only decisions were whether or not to pass matters for decision up the line, or suppress the initiative and avoid the issue altogether. He never made a decision himself. After some months of frustration when nothing was being decided, I planned a different set of tactics. I started feeding him with trivial points which required decision by a certain date, i.e. the details of a conference agenda and the menu for the dinner. As predicted, these were passed up the line for decision until his boss became irritated. I then added some other items connected with these dates, but gave him the information in a way that was certain to make his boss ask some questions. For instance some marketing data, but not all of it; some conclusions from research, but not all the reasoning. Sure enough, my boss's boss asked the questions which my boss could not answer and for a month or so he was a shuttlecock between me and his boss. Eventually the big boss suggested that I should go to him direct and explain, which I did, in terms which at that session were lucidity itself and immediately understood. This episode doubtless contributed to the decision to retire my boss, who went a few months later. It had the effect of freeing up the process of decision making which was good for the business, and therefore such a ploy could be justified.

Another man I worked for was completely hooked on behavioural science, and his whole attention could be absorbed at any time by an article from the Massachusetts Institute of Technology, or a quote from a fashionable exponent of organisational behaviour. He became so obsessed with this substitute for management that his grip on the business and grasp of essential facts, which as Chief Executive he should have had readily to hand, loosened in an alarming way. He started asking the same question of the same people up to three or four times prior to a meeting with his boss and carried with him all the written plans of all his subordinates because he could remember nothing. As it happened, he was a good friend and I was not inclined to provide him with partial information which would have led instantly to his proving his inadequacy beyond all doubt. He became so dependent on the few subordinates he trusted that he dared not let them go on to higher or different things, and in the end it was this additional failure to develop his bright people which was the fatal cause of his downfall.

One fact was certain – if I or one or two of his other trusted subordinates had withheld our help, he would have fallen much sooner. If ever the power of managing the boss was demonstrated it was in this case. He was utterly reliant upon the continuing support of his managers, because he knew we were aware of his uncertainty and weakness and had retentive memories for some his more damning and idiotic "Quotable Quotes" of the past.

In his case, our rabbit gardens were quite adequate. He would not venture beyond for fear of a snare or even a shotgun. He had made the mistake of surrendering his own management style, which was inclined to be manipulative, to an ever varying set of experiments revealed by a succession of behavioural scientists. No sooner had number 10 style been understood and communicated to the top two layers of management, than he abandoned it for number 11. Further down the organisation, numbers 6 to 9 were still being assimilated, and the result was progressive confusion and eventual chaos.

Most managers have their special themes, beliefs or obsessions, and it is as well to be an appreciative audience, at least until you start to hear the gramophone record round again. Let him exhaust his repertoire and show you what he considers to be important. You discuss with him those areas of your business in which he specifically wishes to be kept informed. The first time you do this there may be a mixture of those areas in which he really is interested and those he feels the need to discuss in order to show awareness and alertness.

The second time you discuss it there will be a recurrent theme of those in which he is really interested and, perhaps, a different set of image builders. You can then pick out the real interests. He will appreciate this and warm to the relationship, because he will see you coming out to meet him, and will probably reciprocate by leaving to you other areas which you have indicated you fully understand and are quite capable of handling. One hears of relationships between a man and his boss which result in continuous conflict. Every meeting they have is another bout of unarmed combat where each is trying to win something. This can never really work to the benefit of the subordinate if he relies upon the boss for his growth and promotion. It will end with the man and his boss parting company, probably in stressful circumstances which are unpredictable and therefore damaging. For every man who, after slamming the door and storming out of the business, makes good as the result of a new start, there are ten who regret at leisure that they did not control their destiny more effectively.

One essential obligation on you in achieving freedom by a well planted rabbit garden, is that your boss is never caught out by his boss as a result of lack of information from you. If your boss is confronted with a problem from above on which you should have briefed him but did not, and worse still, you told one of his colleagues and not him, then you will have done him a disservice. He will have incurred the wrath of his boss and that is unnecessary and unfair. As part of your good relationship you should keep your boss out of trouble from above, or from customers and colleagues, by tipping him off when trouble is brewing so he can be prepared and well informed when confronted. The more he lets you get on with your job without interference, the more you reward him with candid communication and a warm relationship. If he steps beyond the rabbit garden without justification, you can then allow the temperature to fall a few degrees and make him work hard to keep his own boss off his back. It is as important to let him see the benefits of warmth as the disadvantages of cold.

When he asks you for information in response to a request from above, your attitude should be 'can do' and 'will do'. Response should be accurate, rapid and willing. If you can develop your own style of layout and phrasing, his boss will soon recognise your work and note whether your boss gives you credit for it or takes the credit himself. The fact that every time information is asked for which affects your department, it is forthcoming in a way which demonstrates your competence and goodwill will not go unnoticed. Let your boss answer the question why his other subordinates take longer to respond, and are less efficient when they do. If he is any good, he will give you the credit for your work. It does you more good to respond in this way than to drag your feet, unless you are deliberately pursuing that policy for good reason.

A technique that has been used on me as a boss in the past, is one of inducing mind-boggling boredom through long and involved narrative, delivered slowly, with the end of the sentence obvious from the half way point, yet still every step is taken. The individual concerned was a long-serving manager who was good at his job and more or less turned in the results predicted. His technique was natural to a large extent, but he was no fool and noticed its particularly frustrating effect on me. Consequently I could never get away quickly enough. If you asked him a question, you regretted it after the first three minutes of the answer, and anyway I neither wanted nor needed to know that much about it. I was never quite sure who the joke was on, but it really did not matter because he seemed to produce the same results whether I offered my help or not, or whether I listened to him for five minutes or for a stupefying hour.

When I ran a sales force, which I did for many years, I spent a good deal of time out with the salesmen visiting the customers. Among others, I used to visit grocery shops, and one particular salesman used to put years on my life. He would enter the shop armed with his stiff-backed order folder which was over two feet long. So that the customer behind the counter could see better he would swing his book round and knock a pile of tins onto the floor. Then, flustered and apologetic, he would bend down and pick them up, and the eggs would crash down as he backed into them. I used to have to go out and sit in the car while the mayhem was in full swing. Whether the performance was contrived for my benefit or not, the deterrent effect was severe enough to put him on my less frequent visiting list.

The use of repellents, contrived or not, is a way to keep unwelcome attention at arm's length. At home, if you dislike do-it-yourself you make sure that early attempts are worse than your wife could do herself. The pictures slightly crooked, the shelf that falls when half-filled – nothing dangerous, just clumsy, will lead to your being asked less and less as time goes on to do any more. It's not only the washing-up and the do-it-yourself that you never seem to get quite right, but in business there are times when it pays to be thick as well. There is the pressure from the buyer for extra discount, the bait he dangles which you do not take, or the supplier who wants earlier payment or a better price.

In the same style it is possible to present innocence in a significant way. There was a farmer who had tried most of the conventional ways of keeping trespassers out of his field, including 'Beware of the Bull', which a quick look proved was permanently absent. Eventually he put up a notice cautioning 'Beware of the Agapanthus' and had no further trouble.

The concept of the rabbit garden is a useful part of boss management, for if it succeeds it means you have assessed your boss accurately, and you can then set about using this containment and intelligence to achieve results and build your career.

You must establish a base from which to advance and this is one way to do it, for if you are constantly in a state of turmoil with an unfettered, untamed boss calling all the tunes and with all the initiative, you are always reacting and never initiating. It is the initiator who succeeds and the reactor who gets passed by. The initiator is the master of his own destiny. He is the one who is unafraid and can pick and choose who he works for. He is not to be bullied and pushed around for he is competent, hard working and determined. Your boss must at least be given credit (after all, how did he get there in the first place?) for being able to distinguish between the initiators whom he should encourage, and the reactors whom he might ignore or kick, if he is that sort of boss, with less fear of reprisal.

The rabbit garden has nothing to do with the hostile freezing out of the boss, if it is to work. It is not a weapon of war and attrition, for that would be counter-productive in the end if the boss has anything about him at all – and if he has not then why are you working for him? There really is no time, if you are going to build a successful career, to get bogged down in futile conflict which leads nowhere. But keeping order while you get on with the job is quite another matter.

5. Always Choose your own Battle Ground

The man who reacts to his boss in a thoroughly predictable way forfeits an important degree of initiative. It gives a boss a sense of power, a relief from tension, an outlet for aggression to be able to induce predictable reactions in those who work for him. It means he can call the tune whenever he wishes, and in such a relationship you will be wary and defensive. This is an undignified position.

It needs the right frame of mind to detach yourself from the puppet string and develop a drive of your own. A good start is to practice not reacting at all in situations where you would hitherto have performed predictably, maybe to your disadvantage. The use of nil reaction can be devastating, particularly when a response of ego building adulation is expected, or when the boss is over reacting in the use of coercion or power. If you just sit there impassively he will be nonplussed – he will be looking for a signal.

You then politely change the subject, or refer to some point that has been made earlier, and take up the discussion from that point. Your boss will unexpectedly have failed to switch you on, and he will think about his effect on you, and try to tune into you instead of taking you for granted.

Nil reaction is a very valuable negotiating weapon. One of the best negotiators I ever knew used to think out his proposition for purchasing a company, rationalising an industry, or introducing a cooperation agreement, and would put that proposition clearly and lucidly to the meeting. He would then sit and stare quizzically at a spot in the middle of the table and give no sign whatever in response to the other side's reactions. They would then enlarge or alter their proposition, and again there would be no reaction. It was positively embarrassing to be at these negotiations, for good manners alone would seem to require a measure of civil recognition of effort. After what seemed an interminable time, and usually after a particularly banale contribution from the other side, our negotiator would come alive and say he would like confirmation that this latest point was to be taken as their answer to his proposition. This would cause further confusion and a renewal of muttering. He would then rise and say that as it looked unlikely that any further progress was going to be made he would depart, but if they were able to come up with anything positive perhaps they would let him know. Otherwise he had nothing to add to his opening statement. Usually he would get part way to the door and be asked to sit down again. At this stage he had all the initiative and it was his proposition that continued to be the focus of the discussion.

There are times when nil reaction can merely feed the boss, already in full cry, with the belief that you are dumbstruck in awe, and this just makes matters worse. At such times it is probably better to restrain yourself and do nothing to enhance the boss's initiative. For at that moment he knows what he is getting at and you do not. He may well have stage managed the whole episode and be counting on a fight to complete your rout. It is his battlefield and he has all the advantage.

It is bad enough when you are confronted with this situation in private session, but it is worse still if you are singled out in public for this sort of attention. There is then the added problem of an audience who, friendly or hostile, will do little to help you weather the storm.

A man for whom I once worked, who was and indeed still is, a dynamic and highly competent manager behaved quite differently in public than he did in private. He was a most helpful and supportive man and, once you had proved yourself, a good friend and teacher – that is in a one to one situation. In a meeting, however, he would become a hard hitting demolisher of one selected member, and all others would be encouraged to witness this blood sport and admire the flushed victor. One had to learn to keep out of conflict in public, but to pursue plans in individual sessions. This boss was very sensitive to opinion and clearly regretted his compulsive public power display. He would try hard and genuinely to re-establish a rapport in private and if you were wise you chose this route. On the few occasions when I felt it necessary to go on the attack, I always did so in private at a moment of my choosing, and never in reaction to his heavy hand.

The golden rule is never to threaten your boss. If you have reached a stage where a real boil-up is called for, there is no point in having a slanging match which will end with your boss asking you what action you propose to take if you are so dissatisfied, or alternatively your threatening to resign. Your boss must in the final analysis assert his authority, and it will be upheld by his boss for the sake of order and discipline. I have always called the bluff of any subordinate of mine who has pursued this tack. If he gives me an ultimatum, he never wins whatever the inconvenience or repercussions.

If you have reached the stage where only a confrontation will clear the air, you should choose your moment to have the confrontation and be sure to have secured a position of strength. It is no good telling your boss you are interested in an advertised job in the hope he will instantly persuade you not to take it, unless you have actually landed that job. First get another job, then hold your confrontation. The more unexpected the confrontation the greater will be its impact on the boss, and if you do clear the air so you can continue to work for him, you will do so on a totally different plane. You will have determined what a[illegible] his and his boss's feelings towards you and your caree[illegible] and you will have registered clearly that you a[illegible] puppet; that you are quite capable of restraini[illegible] tions until you are quite sure it suits you, and [illegible] be taken for granted.

It is essential in the aftermath of such an [illegible]

settle down to wholehearted pursuit of your business objectives again. You will quickly forfeit the new found respect if you gloat and exploit your initiative in a way that challenges your boss's authority. You do not need to rub his nose in it. He will be quite sensitive enough on the issue as it is. The better your work and wholehearted dedication, the greater will be the boss's care that he does not jeopardise it again. Furthermore, the relationship between you and your boss will be of new interest to his boss. He will start to interpret the feedback he hears about you and study your boss's advocacy for fairness or prejudice. He will learn as much about your boss as he learns about you and this will do you no harm at all.

Perhaps one of the main contributory factors to the need for your confrontation is the suspicion that your boss tells a different story about you upwards, to the impression he gives you. Doubts about the fairness of his advocacy will cause you to question your career prospects and make you jumpy and frustrated, or worse still, apathetically resigned to the fact that you are not going to get as far as you had hoped.

Choosing your own field of battle will help you test this situation as nothing else can, but you must pick the issue where right is on your side. That issue may be interference, unfairness, lack of help when you need it, lack of consistency or just a plain piece of perfidy. If you have not got a genuine case, but merely appear to be engineering a confrontation for the purpose of extortion, you are unlikely to win the war, even if you win the battle. You will have shown yourself to be casting your net outside the business and selling to the highest bidder.

You need to gain from a confrontation the freedom to achieve results in your own way, with a supportive and helpful boss pursuing your career growth in a way you have mutually agreed.

It is important to know who your friends are, and just as important to know whom you cannot trust. There will usually be someone in the business stirring it for you, but then there will be others who will support you when justi-
-d in doing so. Your boss will be conditioned by what he

hears about you according to his own values. If he is a results man he will discard as irrelevant gossip that has nothing to do with results. If he is the sort of boss who uses people and situations for his own ends, he will use the network as he pleases.

One headmaster of a school had an uncanny knack, or so it seemed, of knowing what was going on among the pupils almost before they knew it themselves, and was asked how he did it. His method was to assemble a group of pupils, soon after the start of each term, and accuse them forcefully and with the prospect of dire consequences of some breach of the rules. The united silence would be broken as he picked on each one in turn and accused him or her until he found the informer he was looking for. This wretch under the steely lash of accusation would blurt out "It wasn't me, it was him". From then on the headmaster had his source of information, and any sign of it drying up could always be reversed by his threatening to draw the conclusion that the informer was himself the culprit.

The willingness to 'tell the boss' is usually present in one or more executives in any business, and the more remote the information from his own sphere, the safer he feels in bearing the tales. Some bosses encourage and enjoy such a source. Probably they will not have much respect for the informer but such creeps have their uses, so in some atmospheres they are probed and encouraged.

Awareness of this gnawing and burrowing in the woodwork is a basic essential in business, and it is sensible to deny such termites the satisfaction of being able to tell your boss anything of consequence that you have not already told him yourself. If you also refrain from behaviour which will fuel the ever eager tale mongering, you can then afford to ignore the activities of those with insufficient positive work to do, and let the next reorganisation sort them out. There is nothing to be gained from politicking and pussyfooting around the corridors of power on your own account. This merely uses up valuable nervous energy which is better directed at the achievement of results in the business. Furthermore, if you gain a reputation for politicking you will probably be mistrusted by everyone, as they will never know who you are going to talk to next, nor what you are going to say. It is better to keep out of the jungle and rely on results and good relationships based on consistency and integrity.

One sure way to conflict with your boss is for him to hear something which you should have told him from a source other than you. He will strongly suspect that you have said other things which he has not yet heard. Maybe he has projected the results from your area of the business in a rosy light and yet knowing this is not accurate, you have not discussed it. He may deliberately have decided not to publicise a problem, which you then discuss elsewhere to his discomfiture and embarrassment. He is entitled to your support and consideration and should not be let down in this way.

One of the bonds that grows between boss and subordinate is mutual support in times of difficulty. He may be good at containing his own pressure and if so you will know that much of what you tell him stays between you. This can be a comfort if you have dropped a clanger which you would prefer should go no further. The belief that if he says a matter will go no further he means it, can be a source of support. In return he will expect you to keep confidences. If he tells you something when letting off steam or when depressed or elated and asks you not to repeat it, then you should never do so, whatever the temptation to demonstrate the degree to which you are in his confidence. The trust he puts in you and which you put in him must withstand the temptation to talk elsewhere, or it will not last.

The boss who can give you this level of consistent support gains, and deserves great effort on his behalf. The degree to which individuals work for other individuals has been played down over recent years, as the greater glory of the Corporation, the State or the team has taken over. But there is no bond like the one between two individuals dedicated to helping each other succeed consistently and genuinely. You only reach this relationship, however, if it has been forged in bad times as well as good, and this means both parties will have confronted crises singly or together, and almost certainly will have confronted each other honestly and emerged with renewed mutual respect.

Support from then on can extend from the quiet absorption of the other's bad patch, to wholehearted publicity of each other's successes. Unfortunately, some relationships between boss and subordinates can result in the opposite.

There is the story of a traveller who came upon a mouse frozen to the point of death. This kindly man picked up the mouse and placed it in a cow pat to revive in its warmth. In due time the mouse recovered and started to squeak. A passing wolf heard the noise, dug in the cow pat and ate the mouse. The moral of this story is that if you are in the mire, don't shout about it, for it may be your friends who drop you in it, and it may be your enemies who dig you out!

Choosing your own battle field implies that you have the initiative to achieve your aims. In less contentious matters than confrontation it is also valuable. Knowing the moment to raise a matter to achieve a positive response is half the battle. If your boss is on edge or preoccupied with demands from above, the last thing he will want to tackle is a complicated or controversial proposal requiring a decision. He probably needs to be left alone and you should have the sensitivity to do so. If he has just had a difficult session with his financial colleagues or his boss, he may need a chat or a sympathetic ear.

Knowing the right time to act is the one factor which has distinguished success from failure through history. If King Canute, for example, had been sitting on the beach when the tide had been going out, he would have been a national hero. Many a politician has gained popularity and advantage by seeing which way the crowd was running and leaping in front with the cry of 'follow me'. He has to keep doing it, particularly if he has no policies which can be persuasively enduring enough to turn the crowd in his direction and keep it there.

The boss's habits and temperament will help you determine the right time to act. The really exceptional boss will be able to handle anything at any time, unless he is under extreme time pressure. If you work for this sort of boss you are fortunate indeed. I have known those who fit this category and it saves time and the diversion of creative energy which is better spent developing the business. During office hours the boss's lunch time habits may indicate that the mornings are better than the afternoons for discussion of serious matters. An open ended chat at the end of the day, can establish a rapport in a more relaxed atmosphere than a meeting squeezed in between meetings and phone calls. Your aim should be to establish a relaxed and friendly atmosphere through which mutual information can flow.

Accessibility is one of the keys to a good relationship between boss and subordinate. If there is a problem it can be helpful to know where he is, and be able to telephone him and discuss it. This may be at the weekend or at home during the evening. The problem which must wait until office hours, the right mood of the boss or the conclusion of his overseas trip, is the one where almost certainly the right moment for dealing with it will have passed. If you have to undertake days or weeks of conditioning before you can bring a matter up with a reasonable chance of it being discussed rationally, then there is an emotional or behavioural problem getting in the way of the action. That can only be bad for the business and should be sorted out without further ado.

This accessibility should not be used necessarily to discuss everything as it comes into your head. There are those potential problems on the horizon which require thought or planning to avoid or confront and which may never materialise. There is no point jumping at shadows and inviting your boss to do the same, for you will then find yourselves involved in discussion on matters which take the eye off the more urgent and inevitable front burner problems.

The constant wrestling with business problems, in and out of office hours, becomes a feature of the life of those who climb the ladder. The ability to foresee problems and head them off, or go out to meet them, develops through intelligent anticipation. This requires the courage to face the problems head on, and the ability to take decisive action when it is required. There is a marked difference between problem seeking and problem solving. With the former, one's attitude to the status quo is that it is suspect. Hence it needs to be changed because it needs to be improved. This sets off a chain of events which makes for movement and decisions, and as the pace hots up, for firm and resolute management. Problem solving implies the reception of problems as they come at you, and until and unless they do, the situation is normal. In some occupations this is quite reasonable. An airline pilot for example will try to keep the situation normal, and really earns his money on the rare occasions when there is a crisis and he has to use his skill and training to deal with it.

In business, such a frame of mind will place you behind more thrusting competitors who tackle their costs, new product development and organisational structure with more creative vigour, always seeking to improve efficiency. An executive's job should have a strong element of this thrust and challenge, although many seek the quiet life, keeping their jobs ticking over until retirement releases them from the shafts.

The speed of events which you whip up by your own restless thrusting, needs to be understood and accepted by your boss with enthusiastic support. He will be under pressure as things start to move, and the more traditionally minded in the business, resist and complain. It will be much easier for you to keep the initiative if he is with you in the pursuit of the overall strategy, and supports your tactics to the point of wanting to push you faster than you had planned to go. This way you know he is assisting the impetus of what you are trying to do, and you do not have to waste time dealing with him as if he were a brake on progress. If he is the dragging sort of boss then you should analyse why. Is it his own lack of courage or his problems with his own boss, or does he just want a peaceful life until he retires in five years' time?

Whichever it is, you will need to challenge it, and assembling the facts is the best way to do so. If you can show for example, that you have less productivity, lower margins, lower return on capital and so on than your competitors, you are inviting him to accept that your business should continue in this way or improve. If the business is well run there will be no way he can prevent you from publishing the strategy. Having produced an eminently sensible strategy supported by objectives to be met in a stated time, he can only fight your logic with emotion or politics. And why should he want to do that when others can see that what you are pursuing is right? Your skill is to get him to identify himself with this winning formula – and it is not difficult – and then work with him as you pursue it.

The clearer it is, the easier it is to avoid diversion and emotional contributions. "I thought we had agreed to pursue these objectives – that is what I am doing – what are you trying to do boss?"

Managing your boss does not imply the need for combat, nor that he is malign. It is the requirement of all those who wish to create for themselves a base from which to fulfil their career potential.

6. What Does your Boss Think of your Efforts to Manage Him?

Whilst you are pursuing your attempts to manage your boss, it would be wrong to believe that he is innocently unaware of what you are trying to do. He probably does not know the full extent of your thinking, but he will compare you with others who work for him and note some sharp differences. He will not be inexperienced in the art of boss control himself, for he has managed to get to his present job and he will, if he is any good himself, appreciate your thrust and single minded determination to achieve results with the minimum of interference and the maximum of cooperation from himself.

Almost certainly you will be above average if you can achieve results and manage your boss. The fact that you are, means he can turn his attention to those who are not. If the span of control is right, your boss will have six or eight or perhaps more reporting to him, depending on their calibre and occupation and the frequency of contact required. If he has less than six you can expect more involvement because he must make a job for himself, and a rabbit garden is particularly vital to you.

The best way to understand how your boss feels is to view yourself in relation to your own subordinates. They will all be different and varyingly successful in performance. They will each treat you in a different way and you will reciprocate. With one or two you will have an easy relationship, for you know they understand their jobs, their objectives and your mind. It follows that you do not want to get too involved in their affairs.

The fact that they know how you think, how to get your approval and support, should be a source of pleasure and fulfilment to you. It will give you satisfaction to speak well of them, and to tell the world that you have some good people working for you – it is a compliment that they are prepared to work for you and enjoy doing so. You will feel flattered that they have taken the trouble to analyse your style and pay you the compliment of getting to understand you. You are unlikely to resent the fact that they do not want interference, providing they keep you accurately informed.

Some of the methods used on you by your subordinates, which they think are subtle and undetected, will be obvious to you, if only because you have used them yourself and probably still do. But you have, we hope, the discretion and wisdom to understand that if you are more clever than those around you, then you are clever enough not to show it. There is a fair measure of gamesmanship between a boss and his subordinate. Each will pay out the rope at different times, and it will not be too clear which has the initiative, but that is no problem. The fact that the subordinate has the confidence and drive to make the pace when he can, is one of the greatest measures of support any boss can have.

There are, as we will all have experienced, bosses who do not welcome initiatives by their subordinates for this challenges their peace of mind, or threatens to eclipse their own projection. The onus is firmly on you to find a way through the barriers put in your path by a leaden footed, insecure or self centred boss, and this we have considered earlier.

A more serious problem is experienced in jealousy by a boss of his subordinates. This can happen with the proprietor of a family business who has a dynastic mission to fulfil and immortality as his motive. He may develop an outsized ego and petulantly resent challenge which is in any way directed at him and which syphons off any of his glory. Furthermore, he will usually be surrounded by those who are reconciled to the realities of the location of power and who know how to fan his ego, who put up mock opposition and back down in the face of his argument, thus fanning his ego all the more. There will probably be one elder statesman who has known him since he was a boy, into whose care he was entrusted by his father, who knows how to modify the excesses and to handle the tantrums. This sort of dynastic boss is an acquired taste, and you would do well to see your employment as transitory, or live with its realities. An ambitious man will usually fall foul of a proprietor boss and will then be fired, out-organised or suppressed. So learn all you can, give all you have, rise to the level where the proud paternalistic view is changing to identification of a potential threat, and move on.

One such boss I knew, although I never worked for him, was the third generation in a business largely built up by his father from small beginnings started by his grandfather. This man displayed many of the petulant habits which one associates with spoiled children. He was rude to waiters, always demanding something that was not available or sending back something that was. He would keep people waiting for appointments but resented being kept waiting himself. He was vindictive when opposed, and needed the soothing advice of a grey haired counsellor who was twenty years his senior and had worked for his father. When one met this pair, and they seemed always to be together, it was distracting to find that either would take up the conversation where the other left off and it was not easy to know to whom one was talking. Some unspoken signal or chemistry between them would indicate that the boss wanted to take over, and his counsellor would then blend into the background with a chameleon skill, to emerge again on cue. He also fixed the drinks and the itinerary. These two had flown over from the U.S.A. to London to give me the final interview for the top job in the U.K. The boss for whom I would be working was to become the European boss for the company, and he was a man for whom I had respect and would willingly have worked. When I saw the top people, however, I refused the job, and the big boss was so furious that the European chief could not persuade me to take it, that he used this as the basis for removing him.

It was as much the random nature of this big boss's judgement as any other aspect which turned me off. To manage him you had to manage his counsellor also, and that one was not going to do anything for me that would put him in conflict with his boss. One was also as likely to be judged by the quality of the entertainment at the night club and perhaps afterwards, as by the more normal criteria of business performance.

The subordinate most likely to make his boss feel uneasy is the one who is unreceptive. You must know yourself the nag you experience when you are not sure you have made yourself understood to your subordinates, and whether this is due to general thickness or bloody-mindedness. This will tempt you to check up, and if you find a wall of silence or frustrating difficulty in getting at the facts, you will feel unable to count on this man as a supportive member of your team.

Maybe this subordinate is just playing nil reaction for a while, and for a reason which he believes is in his own general interests, in which case the boss can pay out the rope until he finds where it is leading, or pull on it sharply to let him know he is still on the other end. It may be deeper than this however. The subordinate may have reason to keep his boss out because he himself does not know what is going on, or maybe he does know and does not wish the boss to find out. Possibly there are some unwholesome relationships in the picture or he has a behaviour problem.

A boss faced with this situation can try several methods of dealing with it. He can confront the issue and assert his authority, with or without threats of wrath and action to come if the problem continues. He can make an organisational change and introduce an additional subordinate who will report to him quite openly, probably in a specialist or staff role, thereby giving him another line of feedback. Some might even search around in the background for an informer who will creep to him directly or indirectly, maybe through his secretary.

This latter situation is not uncommon and it causes a great deal of trouble. It is your duty as a boss to keep yourself well informed, and this should be done through those who report to you. But if one of your subordinates finds out you are checking up on him through a third party, then the suspicion becomes mutual, and his nervous energy is diverted to protecting his back rather than to pursuing his objectives. A good working relationship between you will avoid this sort of situation. For if you do not like or trust him, you will find a way of causing him anxiety because that is what he is causing you.

Your boss is ill advised to try to cultivate an informer/distorter because it is certain you will find it out shortly. You will know this is going on if your boss keeps on raising points with you which are known, you believe, only within your command. You then get suspicious, and narrow down the possible leak, and test it by telling each suspect something in confidence which you will recognise when it comes back, which it surely will, via the boss.

I had a boss who tried it on me once. He had a close relationship with a manager below me in a company to which I had just been appointed, and kept raising points with me which were obviously being fed. I located the leak, sent for this manager and said if he wanted to go and work for my boss he could do so anytime, but while he was working for me his only contact with my boss would be via me. There was a strained silence for three weeks and then my boss asked the informer why he was no longer talking to him and heard what I had said. There then followed a major row, in which I played a leading role; this cleared the air and the informer departed.

Whereas such practices are to be deplored, there is much to be said for a boss getting to know the people who work for those who report to him. Just as you need to get to know your boss's boss, so your subordinates need to know your boss. If your relationship is right with your subordinates, not only will they tell you what they have been asked by, and what they have said to, your boss, but you will not mind much if they do not. If your boss respects you, he will be very careful how he handles his relationships with your subordinates, for if he oversteps the mark he knows there will be a reaction from you at a time of your choosing. He will tell you of his contacts with them so the atmosphere stays healthy.

You probably have among those who work for you at least one creep, who is inclined to tell you what he thinks you want to know, and will take every chance he can to ingratiate himself with your boss. I find with these people, assuming there is a good reason to keep them, that you need to establish clearly what you expect from them and make sure you get it. The tedious process of cutting through all the waffle intended to please you so you can get to the truth, prevents the formation of a trusting relationship. Ironically it is often the man who is always the diplomat, the sensitive reader of the boss, trying to keep the temperature on an even keel, who thinks he is the best boss manager. In my experience the opposite is just as likely to be the case. The boss confronted by someone always trying to soothe him will be contemptuous and suspicious.

Conflict and tensions are essential to achievement. This conflict should be of ideas, however, and not of behaviour. When two people turn their minds to arguing about an idea, the probability is they will come up with a better solution than either would have achieved individually. Gilbert and Sullivan would never have produced the same quality and quantity of work if they had been soft and pacifying in their relationship. It is impossible to play the violin unless there is tension in the strings, or to shoot a catapult unless the elastic is stretched.

So it is with achievement through people in business. There needs to be a thrusting, full blooded pursuit of goals, and pat ball between boss and subordinate is no way to get there. A challenging and demanding atmosphere is not easy to work in if you want a quiet life, but it is essential if you want to stretch yourself and realise your potential. A boss who will be good for your career is a challenging one. He will stretch you and test you until you prove you can stretch yourself and are several jumps ahead of him. When he asks you to do something, you should do it willingly, speedily and effectively if you agree with it. Most of his subordinates will require chasing and will get more unwelcome attention as a result.

You must earn the right to independence by performance and trust, and this is the other side of the coin in successful

boss management. If you are doing your best and yet your boss interferes and involves himself to the point of your frustration and diversion, you are justified in managing his input with vigour.
"Is there anything I am doing which you would do differently? – Have I missed a trick or an advantage? If so tell me. But if not let me get on with it, and with your support we shall arrive at our agreed destination together".
You lead with your chin in such a reaction but it flushes out whatever is bugging the boss. You can then deal specifically with this issue and put it into perspective.

One problem about being a boss, and having a boss, is to contain interest as such and not have it interpreted as policy, or to be able to discuss and pursue a point and not have it interpreted as an obsession when it is raised more than once. Turbulence under pressure is the enemy of many well laid plans. If reactions to the requirements from above lead to a demonstration of activity below, to please and pacify, then they had better also be related to the objectives of the business, otherwise chaos followed by apathy towards 'policy' will result.

You owe it to your own team to contain or filter the pressure you are under, so you limit confusion and turbulence to the minimum. This takes determination and courage, but if you are convinced you are going in the right direction, and your team understands where that is and why you are all pursuing it, then you must be consistent in the face of pressure. The boss will often test the consistency of his team for his own peace of mind, or because he is himself under pressure which he must deal with. If he finds you enthusiastically consistent yet realistic, in the face of market pressures or uncontrollable external events, he will be prepared to back you more strongly than if he finds you shift your ground every time he growls. In the changing scene all around, you can be the enduring and consistent reference point for enthusiastic pursuit of agreed plans, and he should perform the same role for you. Of such are the best boss/subordinate relationships made.

It is interesting to study the chemistry existing between you and those you get on with, and those you do not. There are some people you feel are 'with' you and with whom you have a rapport, an understanding. They are not necessarily the most gifted or intellectually the best equipped, but they are open with you and support what you are trying to do. It is to these people you would turn if you needed help or effort, and it is to these people you will most likely offer your support when they need it.

You need to work on the chemical reaction you have on your boss. We all find out the hard way how to identify the sensitive areas which cause a programmed unfavourable reaction in other people. Your boss will be just as interested in finding out what switches you on and off. This sizing up process is important, and success in establishing a good relationship will result, because you have both searched for and found the areas of positive reaction, and will manage to keep off the negative areas. Some people get a kick out of inducing predictable reaction in others. This is only a form of showing off, or demonstrating one's puppet master qualities, which is bound to cause resentment and reaction. There are quite enough hurdles in successful pursuit of a man's career, without the additional burden of negative reactions from those who feel the need to get even with you.

The early stages between the new boss and subordinate are perhaps the most testing. Each is on trial and will be testing the ground of his choice. The boss has his authority to assert, and the subordinate wants to come to a working agreement on the boundaries of his independence. Some never make it because they get too preoccupied with conflict and mistrust of each other. Some subordinates make it and then relax, which is fatal. The process is continuous but gets easier as trust grows and results come. It is essential for the successful boss manager to seek freedom to perform and grow, and not freedom to relax.

7. Loyalty

Self-projection and intelligent advocacy will do much to aid a promising career, but the two factors without which it cannot flourish are effectiveness in the job and loyalty in relationships.

The steadfast bond of support and integrity between colleagues, and between boss and subordinate, is the civilising fabric which makes the pressures, tedium, excitements and dangers of one's job tolerable. It adds a quality to the working atmosphere which is apparent when it is there, and unsatisfyingly missing when it is not. The real test of its strength is that it should be there at all times. That means through good and bad. It can be the good times which place it under strain as much as the bad. When results are such as to build the self confidence of the team or some members of the team, this can lead to over confidence and a self centred cockiness which devalues the comradeship forged in adversity. If times are hard, relationships are inevitably under strain as attempts to improve meet heavy weather. Probably the most difficult of all is the strain on loyalties caused by rapid change, where old individual relationships are tested against new demands of performance.

In such a situation the loyalty must be to the success of the enterprise. Yet there will be those who are reluctant to change, or sceptical about a new direction, and expect colleagues to support their traditional and reluctant views as a continuation of loyalty to old relationships. The problem then becomes one of finding a way to be committed to the future and loyal to those whose job it is to ensure it, whilst trying not to be disloyal to the past and all those associated with it, of which you may very well be one yourself.

The pressures are made worse if you are reluctant to pursue your own beliefs and set about finding some middle ground of giving encouragement to other reluctant colleagues, whilst pretending to be wholeheartedly behind the changes. In the end, this sort of double life will be brought to a head by your being asked to decide in which direction you plan to face. Or more likely, the decision will be taken for you, in that if you are not wholeheartedly pursuing agreed objectives you will not flourish, and your attempts to preserve what you have believed to be old loyalties will prove to be counter productive.

There comes a point when the train leaves the station; either you climb aboard or get left behind. Much depends upon your strength of character and your concern or otherwise to be popular, whether or not you fall for the easy ways of gaining temporary favour with colleagues. Accepting invitations to denigrate your boss or your colleagues to suit someone else's mood or purpose is a sure way to be mistrusted yourself. For if you do it with one, he must be fairly sure you will do it with another, so you cannot be really trusted by anyone. Recruitment into a gang is a certain way to surrender independence. Yet walking alone and holding to what you believe in as your own man, is a way of foregoing temporary popularity and a sense of belonging to the society in which you are accepted. In the long run, if your motivation has been consistent pursuit of clear objectives, undiverted but steadfast, determined and incorruptible, you will be trusted and respected.

Loyalty has much more to do with this long term steadfastness than with ingratiating short term behaviour. It calls for honesty and integrity and that can often mean conflict. To hold to a course means that you also hold it when the going is rough and when you disagree with those who would change it for something less demanding, or more comfortable, or just different. We have constantly to find ways of coming back on course, with the buffeting we get in the business environment, and that is the short term flexibility which every businessman must have. But we owe it to those we lead and to those who trust us, to be consistent about what we are doing and strong in defence of objectives which we have persuaded others to pursue with us.

There is enough challenge to safe arrival at objectives from competition and other external influences, without ourselves wavering from the path because we believe it popular with, or loyal to, colleagues to do so. And if this is true for those with whom we work and for those who work for us, it is equally true in the relationships with one's boss. The mutual trust which exists in all sound boss/subordinate relationships is based upon the knowledge that each will do as he says. So if you say one thing to the boss's face and another behind his back, he will inevitably find out – some helpful colleague will always be ready to tell him – and he will not know which of these things you plan to do.

In return you are entitled to expect similar steadfastness from him. One can usually tell when the boss has been got at, because unless he completely rephrases the words he has heard, he will speak in a language slightly out of character, the source of which the trained ear will pick up. The boss will not be short of advice or commentary about your own area of activity, and it is a test of his loyalty to see how he deals with it. The best way to do it is to be completely open. "Willie was talking to me on Tuesday about this and suggested the following – do you think it's a good idea?"

This gives you the opportunity to demonstrate that you will accept ideas from anyone if they are helpful, and go on to discuss the situation sensibly. Or it gives you the unhelpful temptation to get emotional at this lobbying, and you'll fix Willie. The way the boss deals with this situation comes back to the atmosphere and the pecking order of the business. If he is a strictly no politics man, making it quite clear by his intentions and actions that he does not welcome one colleague stirring it up for another, then there will be much less need to watch your back and wonder who is changing the boss's mind about you this week.

The clearer your objectives, the less you have to deal with unsolicited input. For one thing, every one will know what you are trying to do, and if you are sensible you will have involved them at an early stage. For another, you can test all inputs from the boss or anyone else, by pointing to what you are trying to do and checking to see if it's what the advisers are also trying to do. If not what *are* they trying to do?

There are those who take a delight in office politics and all the intrigue and diversion which it causes. You will inevitably have to employ some sensible and subtle tactics at times to achieve certain aspects of your objectives, but it is well to keep clear of the business politicians. For one thing, they will use you for their own purposes and your interests will be a long way down their lists, if included at all. They will always let you down as they change course, leaving you on a sandbank with the tide going out, and they will drag you into areas of conflict which have nothing whatever to do with your own objectives. If you really have to indulge in that sort of thing to get on in the business, then you ought to leave and join or start a business where competence in achieving results is the criterion of advancement.

Usually it is the weakest member of the team who causes the most trouble. He will try to compensate for his inability to perform, by manoeuvering people for his own purposes so as to achieve status and reward in another way. The boss must identify this weak member who is stirring it, and get rid of him or her, to create the atmosphere in which loyal relationships can develop. One major characteristic of a team of loyal colleagues is that they are all professional and get on and do a job of work that is respected by the others. If the pace is set correctly, there will be no time or energy left over to indulge in stirrings and maneouverings. Competent executives allowed to work in isolation leads to the worst of all situations, because they become contemptuous or jealous of each other. The academic world lends itself to this intellectually arrogant disdain, and for political infighting, a university where a Chair is about to fall vacant takes a lot of beating.

The integrity of one colleague to another, and to boss and subordinate, has to have an anchor point which is more permanent than the temporary hitching posts offered by alliances of ingratiation. This applies to loyalty to an organisation or an institution, as much as it does to individuals. The one-company-for-life man quite likely has an even deeper connection through other members of his family who have worked for the same firm, and identifies with the bosses through their families and parallel ageing. Loyalty over this span has its particular risks, as one's fitness to work in any other atmosphere becomes less relevant with every year that passes after 40. With the business environment changing so rapidly and the pace of technological change accelerating, the sacrifice of staying put gives way to the fear of going anywhere else even earlier.

The line between loyalty and dependence becomes blurred in these circumstances, and the other side of the coin of being respected, or taken for granted, or even exploited can become equally blurred. It is a happier state to combine loyalty with independence of mind and speech, than to combine it with a fearing subservience nourished by the possibility of being cast out into a world in which one is unequipped to flourish.

Reality demands that companies keep up their competence if they are to survive, and those who depend upon loyalty as a substitute for effectiveness in their jobs, can find it is not enough. You cannot pay a shareholder's dividend with it, or invest it in the future. It must follow that loyalty must be to the objective the company is aiming for, rather than to a romantic image of what the company used to be, ought to be, or what some pretend it still is. The onus is on the boss to direct this loyalty to a worthwhile performance rather than respect it only for services rendered. He will get little thanks if the economic circumstances which outdated loyal staff have drifted into, cause him to part company with those same people at a time of their lives when they can turn their hands to nothing else of the same calibre.

Honesty in relationships coupled with dedication to a common cause, is the most enduring form of loyalty. But honesty in relationships puts loyalty under strain. "I had hoped I could count on your support", is a reasonable appeal for a rational objective, but it can easily become an emotional pressure on a man's loyalty to agree to an irrational and selfish axe grinding. To be accused of disloyalty because you disagree with such a course of action indicates that you are being used, and your loyalty is being exploited. Honest feed-back will secure the bonds over time, and the certainty that you will always provide it will enable you to avoid getting caught up in political decisions against your better judgement, because you were too 'loyal' to argue. Loyalty cannot be separated from integrity, and the prostitution of your own judgement and sincere beliefs in the name of loyalty cannot be consistent in the long term.

Furthermore, one is inclined to develop loyalty to a number of people over the years, and yet those people may not get on with each other, so they will put you under strain in their calls upon you. The integrity of your feed-back and consistency of beliefs can act as an anchor in these changing pressures, which would have you gang up on one or other of those to whom you are loyal. Encouragement to such behaviour dries up as soon as it is clear you do not propose to be used. Those who face a dilemma in this matter only do so because they are seen to be fair game for predators. It has a parallel with graft and bribes. Those who never take them are the ones least often offered them, if ever. It is a reflection of outlook and attitude which gives the signal of willingness to be used or abused, as any prostitute will testify – at least so I am told.

Consistent, strong minded loyalty can yield quite exceptional response. The boss whom you have supported with integrity through good and bad times will protect you through difficult patches with fierce determination. This support does much to comfort in the struggle of renewing effort to tackle yet another set of problems, having just emerged from the last one. In the pitiless grind, where the every day courage of leading a team with unflagging energy and conviction is the requisite of a successful executive, the one constant of support from your boss counts for much. He will have his bad patches too, and you will see him in moments of depression and perhaps weakness. His subsequent embarrassment, which may cause him to reassert his strength by a show of authority and over-corrective action, should be received with the same understanding maturity which demonstrates that the bond is sound, and more enduring than any ups and downs of the moment can disturb. When the boss can unburden himself to you and let his defences down knowing you will never exploit it in disloyal chit chat or worse, then you can tell him just about anything with a similar level of trust. These bonds are never secured until both have been through several crises of adversity, separately and together, and emerged to enjoy success as a result of strong and relevant action.

The same will apply to your own subordinates. They are entitled to stout and systematic defense if they are energetically doing their best along the path you have agreed. There is a fine line to be drawn between their assumption that they will be supported for genuine work, and defended for bad performance. The latter has no place in the building of team relationships, for why should most members of the team strive to perform well, if one colleague who fails to pull his weight gets equal treatment? Discipline, based on performance toward agreed objectives, must be exercised in parallel with support through good and bad times, where effort is consistent.

Doubtless Causes and Organisations produce loyal application, but people work for other people as much as they do for abstract Institutions. A leader who can lift the performance of his staff and rally them to a common purpose will achieve results which will surprise most of them. Management has lost an element of old fashioned leadership, as the doctrine of consensus and consultation has become the trend in the decision making process. This move to greater democracy has not favoured the individualist with the strong personality, who has more capacity to inspire than a dozen workers' cooperatives or joint consultative committees. Where managers have become afraid to manage in case they baulk the new power structure, or instructions have to be framed as requests, or are the subject of continual debate, the concept of man leading or being led flounders around in depressing confusion. Energy is devoted to defeating the system. Relationship between colleagues and reporting levels cannot develop bonds of loyalty and support, because the purpose of the enterprise takes second if any place, to the daily tussle for power and influence. Worse still is the situation where management has abdicated leadership to a self appointed militant minority. Where firm direction and steadfast purpose no longer provide the framework, relationships do not develop favourably. Mistrust and diversion fill the vacuum and trouble makers have their day.

The mobile society, and the ever increasing pace of change and obsolescence, have tended to encourage executives to set down shallow, if any roots. In fast developing technologies or specialist fields it pays to move around and keep up to date. The development of executive head hunting has also placed mobility on the advancement slate. Such a fast moving scene tends to work against the development of loyal relationships, although it is likely that key executives will follow a trusted boss or colleague around from firm to firm, to the inevitable accusations of enticement and disloyalty from a succession of ex-employers.

The development of a relationship between advancement and mobility has put a premium on shifting allegiances, and has inevitably devalued long standing relationships in the eyes of those who do not establish them. Also, some who do, question the wisdom of staying put when so much green grass, apparently, is growing out there. That loyalty has taken on the image of one of the old fashioned values as if it were the model T Ford of human relationsips, is an inevitable result of this mobility and changing values of success. It happens in every day life as any product marketeer or supermarket company will tell you. The consumer will shop around, hunt for bargains and switch allegiances for 2½%. It is little wonder that brands of soap powder, choice of eating places, human relationships, choice of airline, allegiance to employer, change of holiday scene all get caught up in the mobile, adventurous, materialistic self interest which has become a feature of life.

Against the lure of these noisy sirens the decent and enduring, profound and mature find it harder to thrive. But when discarded packaging lies in the heap with its unfulfilled promise, one brand has proved to be much like its rival, one unsatisfactory relationship so like the last, then the anchor point remains, and is there for the use of anyone who has the time to notice it in the breathless rush past. The bonds of loyalty endure.

8. Promotion

A man can work diligently in obscurity for years without the active backing of his boss, and be left languishing to the point where it becomes generally accepted that he does that job and nothing else. Those who would have been capable of doing a bigger job, and maybe still are, and who have got stuck, are usually in this position because they have failed to inspire those who could identify them as promotion candidates, and lacked the confidence and drive to move on to another company where they would be more appreciated. These people do not take care of their own careers. They put their trust in the system and believe they will be carried along on the tide to wherever it happens to take them. Such a chancy process will not steer in any particular direction and suggests that the chosen direction is not clear.

There is little we cannot achieve in life if we are determined and single-minded enough. Part of this single-mindedness is to generate the momentum which will carry us forward, and in so far as a reliance upon one's boss is a part of the process then that must also be managed. The skill is to harness all the leverage the boss and the system can provide to carry us forward. To do this each of us must ensure two things:

Firstly to demonstrate that we can perform in the job and are to be trusted. Trust is the relationship between what one says one is going to do and what is actually done. The wise boss will allow for the degree of head wind or side wind that we experience and also for whether we set initial sights high or low.

Secondly, we must establish in the boss's mind that the ability to develop subordinates for promotion is a key criterion in the judgement of his own performance.

The way we tackle this second factor will vary according to the culture of the business. In a large company the boss will be under pressure to review the list of his promotable subordinates who can be written into the Group's succession plans. If the boss's record is poor, in that he never has any names for the list, or the ones he has are poor by comparison with the lists of his colleagues, he will do himself no good at all. It will demonstrate that he is either employing poor people, which if other results are good, is unlikely, or for some reason of poor judgment or insecurity he is leaving the talent off his list.

It is as well to find out whether or not your boss has a good reputation for developing subordinates before you start to work for him. This focusses attention and requires an answer. If the answer is good you have nothing to worry about, assuming you are a suitable candidate. If it is bad then you must work on it and focus attention on this aspect at appropriate moments.

Not only does raising the question of management development give you the opportunity to keep this goal in front of your boss, but it helps the careers of your own bright and thrusting people. Your boss should be asked to recognise this skill in you, and you will have the opportunity to discuss the future of your staff with him, as often as you choose to raise it.

It also gives you the opportunity of making contact with colleagues and becoming known elsewhere in the organisation. If you put up names to fill vacancies and offer to give some background information on the individual to those interested, it helps your own projection and reputation. All businesses are short of talent at some time. In times of expansion and growth the most likely restriction on the business is the lack of available talent to fill the jobs essential to this growth. It is at times like these that your boss's thoughts and his boss's thoughts should turn to you, and you should be ready to accept the challenge if it looks like a real opportunity.

At times of cutback in new investment it is the specialists who will be thinned out first. For example, a research and development executive will find it difficult to develop his span of control, or even keep what he has. In the same way advertising may, wrongly, be cut back in hard times and the business stripped to its main line operations, with a minimum of supporting staff.

There is no reason why the disappearing job should necessarily mean the disappearance of its occupant, providing he or she is seen as a valuable member of the company with potential. He or she needs to be visualised filling a different role. There is a considerable danger in climbing a single specialised ladder, and you owe it to yourself to widen your experience so as to broaden the application of your energies. Most accountants after a while in the profession want to do something else and some succeed in finding another ladder to climb before it is too late. The accountant who can manage people and has the personality to thrust forward rather than to gaze backwards, can combine to good effect the numerate skills with the operative skills required of effective managers. There are some good examples of accountants who have made good outside their profession. Michael Heseltine, and John Barber ex-Leylands are perhaps the two outstanding examples. Then there are the medical doctors who have blossomed out of their specialisation to success elsewhere. Perhaps Dr. Edward de Bono is the best example, and Lord Hill of Luton – the former Radio Doctor and distinguished politician – is another. Numerous salesmen have made the big time such as Lord Stokes and Lord Errol, and scientists – Barnes Wallis, Christopher Cockerill to name two. For every one who has hit the big time there are many less famous, but who nevertheless have the willingness to spread out and grow on a firmer base. Hence we see accountants becoming buyers, buyers becoming salesmen, engineers becoming planners and in time they can move into more general management and occupy top jobs in industry.

Sales and marketing management have a good vantage

point from which to move into general management. That is if the other parts of the business with all the problems of industrial relations, logistics, systems and painstaking development can be digested without blunting their thrusting sharp end skills. The broadening process needs to be a natural development of perceived talent, and not a hedge hopping piece of wishful thinking which takes you out of your element and into an unknown area for which you are neither imminently nor potentially equipped.

If your boss is wise, he will help you in this broadening process, and probably surprise you with some of the suggestions he makes for your career development. This is all part of the process of stretch and challenge. It is desirable to talk about your career and your needs objectively, with someone you trust, who is in a position to give you good advice. If your present boss is that man so much the better, but maybe an ex-boss, or a colleague with whom you get on well, can help you steer your drive for promotion in the best direction. You must take care you do not overdo the bobbing and weaving to catch the boss's eye. If you give the impression your eyes are constantly on the next job, your boss will doubt the diligence with which you are tackling your present one. Furthermore, if you are constantly discussing your promotion, you must expect to be rebuffed, particularly if you have been in your present job for less than say two years, and there are some unresolved problems which your boss is expecting you to solve and continues to wait for you to do so.

I had a sales executive of 26 reporting to me, who came via a take over and believed he was a great gift to the world of business in general, and to my company in particular. He would tell me how he was ambitious to double his salary in 18 months, get a seat on the Board and run a large organisation at the earliest opportunity. Did I know his father was the managing director of a large and very successful company? Every time we met and reviewed performance I was treated to a thinly veiled threat that the work in hand was not sufficiently stimulating, that he was easily bored and could walk out any time and get a more suitable job. This went on for about three months until it was clear there was more wishbone than backbone about him. His customers were complaining of unfulfilled promises and lack of follow through, and performance was bad. The next time we reviewed performance I presented him with my list of dissatisfactions, and we parted company. He joined another company with the promise of a directorship, which materialised twelve months before the firm went bankrupt.

At the other extreme, a manager in his early 50s who was transferred to me had, by all accounts, reached his peak some ten years before. He was thinking himself and others into the belief that he was drifting towards a premature retirement. Yet this man had great creative ideas, sound experience and the ability and willingness to learn. At the age of 55 I put him on the Board and it was as if I had unlocked a flood of new vitality and effectiveness. He was able from that point to give his energies to the pursuit of business goals and be less preoccupied with the frustrated thirst for recognition. He surprised himself more than others by his ability to think through and tackle problems.

Promotion must be earned with full blooded involvement and not grovelled for. The lengths to which some will stoop to ingratiate themselves with the boss are nauseating. I know one man who would leave his office light on at 5.30 p.m. go and play snooker, then return with a file under his arm and a diligent expression on his face at 6.45 p.m. as his boss was walking down the passage to go home. Another would lurk on a bend in the stairs until he saw his boss's car pull up in the morning and then hurry down and pass him, by chance you understand, halting in his dedicated pursuit of some urgent business problem only long enough to gasp a surprised good morning.

This sort of undignified subordinate behaviour is a complete waste of time, for no boss can be fooled for long. If he does not spot what the groveller is playing at, then the groveller's colleagues most certainly will, and they will interpret this behaviour at some inopportune moment which will put the picture firmly on the canvas.

There is much to be gained in cultivating your boss as a friend if you can base the friendship on mutual respect. It can go too far, however. If you have such an affinity with the boss that you wish to work for him and him alone, you are shutting the door on the big wide world. Also no boss-subordinate relationship can be all sweetness and light and if the boss starts pulling his punches because of personal friendship, this will almost certainly work against your best performance, determination to perform without limitation and growing effectiveness. Your cutting edge will be blunted and the absence of conflict and creative tension will sap your divine discontent. Furthermore your dual objective of performing at your peak and managing your boss to further your career, will be blurred.

It is as well to remember that your boss is looking for promotion too, unless he is at the top of the tree or soon to retire, and in order to perform well he will need to develop his subordinates and delegate to them those matters which free him to concentrate on what he considers important. A well tried route to promotion is to work yourself out of a job and be ready to tackle something additional or different. Your boss will therefore be pushing in your direction some matters with which he does not want to deal, and part of the test of your potential will be for him to see you tackle these matters with decision and without bothering him. The capacity to absorb work and pressure, to dominate problems with resilience and resolution are good indicators of further potential.

If you believe you are a good operator and have a clearly identified career objective, you will have nothing to fear in working yourself out of a job. If you do fear doing so you should ask yourself why you believe that other doors will not be open to you if you knock on them. Is what you have to offer so specialised and so narrow that no one else can use it? Are you so dependent on the goodwill of one man or one firm that you are a slave without drive or free will? The risk of putting this to the test is high with a home to keep and a family to provide for, but you never hear of anyone starving to death in the developed world.

If you are desperately clinging to the job you have for fear of not finding another, then your attitude to full blooded commitment will always be restrained by the desire to play it safe. As a promotion candidate you must lack something if this is your outlook. There are plenty of managers in industry who like to minimise risk and who turn in mediocre performance as a result. The promotable candidate is the one who is likely to carry his next job somewhere more exciting than the average. If all he offers is to maintain the status quo then he is not going to advance the cause and the job had better go to someone who will.

The willingness to take risks must be accompanied by acceptance of the consequences if they go wrong, but if you grasp a nettle firmly you are less likely to get stung than if you fiddle around with it. Those who set about their careers with this attitude not only achieve much more, but find opportunities opening up before them which the faint-hearted never see.

In a more extreme way it is said that if you are not afraid of death then you are not afraid of life. Certainly those who distinguish themselves on the field of battle must possess a large measure of this philosophy, and what is business, or life for that matter, if it is not a battle.

The men and women who achieve are in general by no means more clever than those who do not. They use what they have without self imposed limitation and with no check to their effectiveness. They believe in themselves and have unshakeable goals to which they stick through adversity and through the inevitable gratuitous discouragement of the Jeremiahs.

The establishment of clear goals and the belief that you are capable of achieving them does wonders for the sureness of touch you bring to the job in hand. This does not take long to communicate itself to those around you and above you, and therefore you become more valued and less vulnerable. This in turn breeds confidence. Your promotion should be and probably will be the result of positive performance and thrust, and the recognition by your boss of your initiative and effectiveness. You will have avoided defensiveness and actions which are prompted mainly by the boss and your subordinates. Such criticisms that he makes of you will concern actions rather than inactions, and when you have not acted it will be as a result of a conscious decision not to do so, instead of procrastinating inertia which is the enemy of success.

It is a mistake to believe everything must go right in your job to qualify you for promotion. Indeed, if you have not had real problems to sort out, and shown yourself to be capable of facing them with courage and endurance, you could well be passed over for promotion to a tough job because your experience will be incomplete. If there are not enough scars on your back for the toughness required in the next job, you may not get it.

Your boss will have endured and lived through problems and is not judging you by their absence in your area, as much as by your handling of them through people and your attitude. If you accept them, face them, solve them and they stay solved, you are well on your way to demonstrating your courage and effectiveness. In addition, you have to demonstrate your initiative, creativity and ability to dominate events and achieve results.

9. The Wife's Role

Part of the team but seldom part of the act, would seem to be the winning formula for the wife of the successful man. She has the task of keeping his feet on the ground – neither suspended above it at times of enthusiasm nor sunk into it at times of depression. She provides the enduring anchor point around which his career can pivot, growing with him, encouraging and stretching him. To provide the added confidence when it is required and the restoring self respect when he has problems, is the role of stalwart support which no one else can provide.

This level of support is quite different from the nagging, pushing ambition which drives a man to overreach or depart from the path on which he knows he can fulfil himself, so that he develops a frustrated and miserable business existence. This is exceeded only by the misery of returning home to explain to his wife why he has not made as much money as her brother, his brother, the neighbour's husband or the one-armed bandit machine operator who has a new Rolls every year.

It puts a real strain on the husband if he feels he is regarded as a walking meal ticket, always expected to provide the money for the standard of living to which the family aspires. His anxieties and the ups and downs which cause him tension need a sympathetic ear, and encouragement founded on the belief that the family will stick with him if he has a bad run.

To be crushed between the home pressures, which demand continuity of an ever increasing money supply, and the work pressures which require ever improved performance in a changing economic environment, is enough to drive a man to drink, ulcers or worse. The excitement and pleasure of success at work and a warm home and growing family, can turn into a series of ever more burdening threats under which he may sink, from which he may run or which he may transfer to colleagues, subordinates or boss at work, or to his family at home.

The home atmosphere which she creates operates best when the every day worries and problems are on a different scale to the problems at work. Lady Dorothy MacMillan, that great calming influence and wise consort, greeted her Prime Minister husband at the door of 10 Downing Steeet at the height of the Cuban crisis and asked him anxiously if he had heard the awful news. "Is it war?" he asked. "War? No, Alex has failed his exam." Dame Florence Bevin turned away a delegation at the front door at the height of a crisis with the information that Ernest was asleep and she would not disturb him for anyone or anything.

There is a reassuring quality about arriving home with your head full of large scale problems, to be told after the usual greeting that the drain is blocked or a picture needs putting up or the oil man has not been. You may not want to do anything about it but at least it brings you down to earth and keeps your importance in perspective. 'You may be a big shot at the office, Fella, but if you don't mend that plug none of us gets a hot meal tonight'.

If the antidote to your problems is to relate to your wife's, then she has a right to an antidote to hers. To be bounded by the house and the domestic scene with no other interest is restricting, and particularly difficult when the children have grown up and flown the nest. The temptation for her to get involved in your business in exchange is no solution, for it can lead to the sort of pressures you can well do without. If the wives of the executives in a business develop a hierarchy of their own based on their husbands' jobs, watch out. There is nothing to say that the personalities and characters of the wives in any way match their husbands', and a pecking order established on these lines is bound to lead to trouble. If they are well informed on what their husbands think about each other it can lead to indiscretion. If they are poorly informed it can lead to speculation. If wives of executives must meet, let it be at social gatherings with their husbands and then the interplay is contained, anticipated and intermittent. There will be special relationships where one wife's husband has progressed over the years with another's, and a close association has built up based on long standing genuine friendship. This will survive one husband leapfrogging another in status and does not have about it the bitchy parallel structure, where reflected power asserts itself and undercurrents flow.

The boss will probably want to meet your wife and will arrange a suitable occasion. You will then be faced with the problem of how to return the hospitality, and it is well to avoid the painful dinner for four which tends to bring out the potential gaffes and disasters. Jangling nerves put the least relaxed and most artificial behaviour on show, which is the last thing you or he wants to see or demonstrate. It is better to ask the new boss and his wife to a larger gathering, with the company selected to put you and him at ease. In over 20 years I seldom entertained the boss for whom I was working, and I have only entertained those who worked for me with their wives when the whole team was invited, and then usually with others not connected with the job. This way, the development of a relationship with the boss can pursue a business based course without other factors getting in the way. The picture changes again when you sit on a board, with your boss and one or two of those who, wearing one of their several hats, work for you. Board level relationships run closer to that of colleagues with whom you can develop as free a relationship as you wish.

I have a horror of the scene around the boss's swimming pool on a Sunday morning when he holds court, at which his subordinates and their wives take part in some career advancing hinting and pushing. These pressures will show up the husbands in a light which can put them at a disadvantage, or in some way enhance their perceived virtues, in a manner wholly irrelevant to the achievement of results in the business. If tribal gatherings of this type are necessary to get on in the job, then the chances are that you are in the wrong company.

It is only fair to your wife, who bears the brunt of the claustrophobic, repetitive grind of looking after the house, with the worries and sheer hard work of bringing up the children, that she should be encouraged to develop her own interests. And you have to be consistent about it. If she gets involved in voluntary work or local government, evening classes or a hobby, she could well be out some evenings when you are in. It cannot be taken for granted that she can fit in with all your arrangements as you make them. It needs an accommodating frame of mind to give her consistent support to develop her interests, without her feeling guilty that she is not always there when you come home. This may be the very thing that neither wants to encourage. If she is quite content to do the housework and chat to the neighbours or go shopping, fetch and carry the kids and chat to the girlfriends during the day then that cannot be bad. But if the price of it is to involve herself in your business then it cannot be good either.

The problem can be when the wife hears about details of the work and does not necessarily appreciate the sensitivity or delicacy of what she hears. Is it confidential, and if so do you have to say so every time you tell her anything? – if you do she will object to your continued reminders and think you do not trust her not to talk. And what can you say about business that is not confidential somewhere or sometime. It does not help either if, when the wives meet, some of them seem to know more than others and discuss matters quite openly which set your antennae cringing at the ends.

Yet if you are not going to tell her anything, how can you expect her to take an interest in what you are doing? Better her interest be kindled in those things you do together and with the family, and which she pursues and with which you can identify. If your wife can keep a secret she really can help you, for at times she can bring a practical angle to bear on a problem which you would not think of yourself. To be able to discuss a problem and know it stays between you, helps the anchorage.

Some bosses' wives seem to travel continually with their husbands and share much of the inevitable entertaining. Those who do, have to be fairly self-sufficient if they are to avoid being a distraction to the business, which is usually compressed and gruelling on such trips abroad. The occasional more leisurely tour of the outposts, and public relations visits to factories and contacts can cement the business. The proprietor of a consumer goods business was visiting a long standing customer in Glasgow and they got chatting of old times for over three hours. Eventually the meeting broke up and the customer asked how the proprietor's wife was. "She's fine – come and see her, she is sitting in the car" "I'm so sorry I had no idea – I would have invited her in if I had known". "She's quite happy, she has her knitting".

There is something to be said for living some distance away from the place of work. It gives you the chance to unwind on the journey – both ways – and you can develop your own circle of friends without being too closely involved with the people with whom you work. Your wife can appear at prize givings and social functions connected with your work, meet your colleagues and staff and their wives and remain uninvolved if she wants to do so. You miss the local activities and the events which surround the place of work, and you get to know less of the people you hear about.

In a small town, where the firm is the main employer and most of the staff live within walking distance, the strain of it all can be difficult. If the firm is having a rough time and there are layoffs, you are involved at all levels and your life becomes wholly intermeshed with the business. Maybe if you own it, that is inevitable, but if you are employed by it at least you have the option.

A husband and wife in business together must find a particular strain. To see each other all day and after work too must make for a staleness that is good for neither. Yet there are some good and lasting husband and wife business teams. I know a couple who run a public relations business. They are wholly interchangeable in their roles in the firm, creative and efficient. At weekends they go off together to their boat, which seems to spend more time being prepared for sea than afloat. After a weekend in solitude together they resume on

Monday morning, running their business until the following weekend's boatwork.

Another couple I knew were a formidable team. He rose through the ranks of his family business and became chairman of what was then a major group, and she instituted some staff welfare innovations which, when they were introduced, were considered to have been well ahead of their time. To the work force she was counsellor, mother, innovator and inspiration and the wife of the boss some way down the list.

Whether your wife is involved in the business or not, it helps to encourage her to enlarge her horizon as you enlarge yours. If this does not happen the couple grow apart and she cannot compete with the new scope of your job and friends. It can go the other way too. The ambitious, well connected wife who has plans for her promising husband to one day achieve in his own right what she is used to from her father and family, but then he does not make it. "Daddy was a general and I married you as a young lieutenant. You really should have got much further than major by now" is every bit as depressing as "I know we had the sauce bottle on the table when we were first married, and your mother had never taught you to cook, but we have an important customer coming tonight and they don't do that in France."

There are those executives who use their wives shamelessly to enhance their business interests. Some will wear them as a glamorous addition to their own image, use them to distract a client, much as a conjurer does to draw attention away from his sleight of hand.

For the politician the wife's role is very much as part of the team. The average member of Parliament has to visit at least one social event in his constituency every week. Fund raising at such events is the foundation of the financial resources of most political parties. The continual encouragement of the party activists at such events demands attention from the MP's family and certainly from his wife, who has a role to play in encouraging the women. Such a role demands a combination of stamina, a good memory for names, faces, relationships and trivia and the ability to remain detached from controversy or the support of factions. The ability to talk to anyone, to make conversation about anything at any time is a gift which some women possess in strong measure. Most women can talk or gossip, but some can contain this facility with poise and a sense of timing. Such consorts provide substantial support to their menfolk.

One hears of the most incredible capacity for capable achievement from some wives. One matriarch had nine children and ran the family business, having taught herself to read and write. Then all nine children died during an epidemic and she had a further six. At every stage her home was run for the benefit and comfort of her husband.

Margaret Thatcher has insisted, at all stages of her remarkable career, on maintaining the role of wife and has always cooked her family's breakfast and carried out her own housekeeping. It is not easy to identify many similarities in the wives of the successful. Perhaps the most constant thread is that they enable their husbands to succeed, whether they are kept strictly in the background and never appear at all, or are at every conference, foreign tour, office party and flower show. It is the successful operation of the team that counts. It is the pushing strident, discordant wife who does the husband no good. For some jobs she may positively hold him back.

It is interesting to speculate on what sort of wife a man has at home. The Holy Terror at work who is abrasive and difficult would, one might think, be married to a poor cowering little woman who hovers to do his bidding. It is often not the case at all. He behaves the way he does at the office because at home he is treated in the same way. One prize pig I knew was married to a prize bitch and he took it out on all around him at work. I knew a bank manager who always appeared to be a restrained and respectable gentleman in tweeds, with grey hair and a military moustache. Then I met his wife who was a blousy blonde in slacks with a great red gash of a mouth, which with some assistance from lipstick, seemed to extend from her nose to her chin. She could and did swig gin with practised ease and had a fund of stories one might think would have curled the ends of her husband's moustache. He used to take it all with an amused detachment. Just as opposites attract each other, so do those with potential similarities. We must all know couples who grow to look and talk alike. One couple I know are like a pair of parakeets clicking and clucking at the millet seed. They are the same height, shape, colouring and outlook, until one would think they might find difficulty in knowing if they were talking to themselves or each other.

The hard, scheming woman usually causes some form of irregular behaviour as her husband tries to reconcile the constant home and business pressures. Maybe he drinks or has an affair in or out of the office. Many men who make a mess of their home lives make a mess of their business lives too. For others, release through divorce can in its turn provide an outlet for the latent talent to come through and flourish, in a way which might have avoided the breakup had it been encouraged to come earlier.

Unless the wife will be required to play a part in the business scene, and I cannot think of many situations where this is essential, the practice of interviewing the wives at the shortlist stage for the employment of an executive is an intrusion which no business has the right to insist upon. In selecting a parliamentary candidate it has its uses, because she is involved with the constituents as part of the team. Even here, I suspect, it has more to do with finding out what sort of person the candidate is and satisfying some of the women on the selection committee in their curiosity, than to determine how good a member of the team his wife is likely to be. For example, did he marry a barmaid and if so did he have to? Or is she some potty eccentric who attached herself somewhere along his upwards path? Is she going to get in the way or help him along? If the candidate is a woman there is usually less interest in meeting her husband.

The successful tycoon whose career has been a series of risks, excitements and dangers and who after forty years still has his faithful wife at his side with whom to enjoy his remaining years, is fortunate and by no means exceptional. She has probably played a clever and conscious part all the way – knowing when to get involved, and with equally sure instinct when to leave well alone. Supporting through tough times and never distracting when the good times needed equal concentration. Bringing up the family with a sense of values and trying hard not to let them get soft and spoiled on the fruits of their parents' success. Comforting her husband when the children let him down, lifting him out of the dumps when he needed it. Maybe she did not get the same support, and at times had to fight her depression and worries alone, not wanting to distract him at a critical time. The tough, courageous wife and mother is the strength behind many a strong man and the support behind many a weaker one also.

The wife's role is a subtle and sensitive one if played for the benefit of her husband. It has finesse and restraint, strength and consistency when carried out well. It has a discordant and unhelpful effect when used to push and drive her busband for money. The death stroke to a career can be when the wife intervenes with the boss to get her husband promoted. When she uses what her husband has told her about the business to put pressure on the boss, he will be bound to worry about the level of out of office gossip that goes on, and mistrust the husband with an important job, or any job. It is one thing for the boss to manage an executive, but when he has to deal with that executive's wife as well and cannot control her tongue, her spleen or her ambition, he is better off without either of them.

10. Politics at Work

Ask any delegate to a management training course why he is there, and you will touch a nerve. For each one who genuinely believes it is part of a development programme, leading to career enrichment and promotion, there will be three who fear what is going on in their absence. Some will believe they are there to be corrected for faults, others that they ought to be there because it seems to be expected of them. But most of those attending will be worried that some sort of reorganisation is planned or in the process of execution, and it has been arranged to coincide with their absence. There is usually one who is there because he has started to develop some unwelcome behavioural problems and it seemed to be the best arrangement to send him 'away' for a while.

The anxieties set up by such tactics are considerable, yet they are only a symptom of a deep-rooted neurosis shared by many in business about an undercurrent of political manoeuvering. Politics at work is one of the more debilitating and widespread diversions, as manoeuverers and manoeuvered shuffle around the scene exploiting situations at the expense of others, or being pushed about to suit a tide on the flow.

It can lead to the sort of insecurity which makes executives fear to be away from the office, or to go on holiday, because of the advantage their absence gives to those who will stir it. Holidays are then chosen carefully, at a time when the boss is also away, so he cannot be lobbied against you.

The symptoms of a politically active organisation are many. Arguing by memo is one of the more usual. Instead of sensible face to face discussion, there will be a prolonged correspondence with copies to a growing number of observers, with the objective of neutralising the colleague who is most involved, and thus demonstrating how pure and diligent is the memo writer. It is also a symptom of mistrust, to get everything down in writing, so that in the event of a come-back one's detached innocence can be established by further memos referring to earlier correspondence. This "see how clever I am" performance has all the nauseating smugness of those who would rather be right than effective, which kills initiative and enterprise on the altar of bureaucracy. The memo which replaces face to face discussion is the hose which puts out the fires of enthusiasm, the road roller which flattens and erodes enterprise into a flat, unimaginative landscape.

Another symptom is the dotted line on the organisation chart. This indicates that a nettle has failed to be grasped and a compromise arrived at, through indecision or the grinding of an axe somewhere. This has more to do with maintaining the balance of power, an empire, or the status quo, than getting results through accountability.

Every dotted line is a licence to escape decision making. It fudges issues, blurs the edges of accountability and neutralises the parties to which they report, as each will be reluctant to act because no one owns the problem. War lords flourish in this situation, and lack of clear cut responsibility gives the feeling to those who want to pursue it, that out of confusion comes personal opportunity to be pursued without sanction, for the greater gratification of the individual. The effect on others of seeing one part of the organisation excused 'boots' in this way, is either one of resentment, or provocation to join in the anarchy as and when it suits them.

The insidious, subtle conditioning by politically motivated colleagues is the most usual area of attack. Any opportunity to place another in a doubtful light, will be taken as a hint that responsibility for a mix up should really be pinned in that area, but in the interest of good colleague relationship you would rather not pursue it . . . . This followed up by a nose-rubbing public memo, giving a history of your own lily white innocence and drawing the obvious conclusions, can be augmented by taking the opportunity at a meeting at which the boss is present, to offer further evidence which has not been discussed with the victim. He, taken by surprise, can be provoked into reacting to his own detriment and to your further vindication, so that the boss sees how right you are, and how wrong your colleague is.

I have always been intensely suspicious of any manager who stirs it up for one of his colleagues in this way. He is clearly pursuing some motive of his own, which has little to do with any task I have agreed with him, and he is probably diverting attention away from some dubious performance of his own which he would rather did not see the light of day. The attribution of blame is one of the most counter productive of all human relationships. We learn by our mistakes and will not progress if we are punished every time we make one. Indeed if our success rate is 50% we are doing exceptionally well, and are unlikely to add to our score of mistakes and successes if we are punished for everything that goes wrong. The relationship between boss and subordinate has to be forged through the ups and downs of endeavour, and it is up to the boss to form his judgement as to the score. For a colleague to intervene and try to sour this relationship for his own ends is totally unhelpful, irrelevant, uncalled for, and to be dealt with. Yet in many organisations it is either encouraged, or not discouraged. Good operators then divert to guarding their backs instead of performing, to levelling the score rather than working with colleagues. The gamesmanship of getting things done in such an atmosphere is a major factor in the use of nervous energy.

Confronting issues with the parties concerned is the only way to deal with these issues. If you go to your boss with a tale which you hope he will use to your advantage against a colleague, it is devastating to find him lifting the telephone, inviting that colleague to come and join the meeting, and then asking you to repeat what you have said. In a clean atmosphere this only has to be done once to stop the insidious time wasting. But where the boss himself is caught up in the cross-fire of political intrigue, his need for ammunition and evidence may be such that he welcomes this source of supply, so he can use it to his own advantage in due course.

If you cannot operate and succeed in such an atmosphere, then it is best to get out and go where your skills as a manager can be pursued and politics avoided. There are plenty of opportunities to use political skills, either outside the company or for the company's benefit, towards competition or the government, who may be interfering in your business, but in your place of work it is bound to be against the best interests of your company.

Sometimes you have to give a political colleague a lesson, which in itself may be classed as politics, but at least it is geared to the removal of diversion so you can get on with the job. I had a colleague at one time who was clearly working against my interests by stirring it continually with our joint boss. I waited until I had a good case and then went to see the boss to say I really had to reduce the profit forecast I had agreed with him because he was clearly not committed any longer to the support I needed to achieve it. This provoked shock and surprise until I pointed out that he was being conditioned to deny me this help by my colleague and he must really make up his mind if he was with me or not. The insidious interference was stopped forthwith, and my colleague was exhorted to get on with his own job and watch his tendency to turn each instruction from the boss into a debate. Once such a breakthrough is achieved, any temptation to repay the erstwhile stirring colleague is to be strictly avoided. A whole new relationship will follow confrontation if a path of rational action is pursued without sanction. To enable people to make mistakes without retribution and with forgiveness, is one of the most enriching of interpersonal relationships. If your own motives are elevated and visible, you will always defeat those who are mean and self interested, if you have the courage to be honest under pressure, consistent when provoked, and prepared to stand your ground when being pushed around.

A clean style of management has to start somewhere. You may think you are a mug for refusing to join any gang or clique, while you preserve your loyalty and pursue your objectives, but you will win in the end. If the company you work for cannot use what you offer, then there will be plenty who can, so push off and leave the heaving squabblers to their games of cops and robbers and pursue your career where they can be forgotten. Usually the less effective the manager, the more he will have to contribute to diversionary behaviour. If you analyse those who are the most politically active in a business, you will find the thread of personal inadequacy, or managerial incompetence, or both, running strongly. The colleague who tries to recruit you to a gang is after something not in the interests of your boss or yourself or the business. If your boss is no good, then you must decide for yourself what you do about it. You do not need some personal axe grinder to use your concern for his own ends.

A difficult situation to cope with is where your boss does not get on with his boss and tries to use you to pursue his battle. You will be encouraged to send him point scoring memos and reports, which he can use as evidence against some policy which the boss's boss is trying to pursue. I have worked in an atmosphere where my boss was trying to get his boss removed in favour of another at the time of some reorganisation. My boss would then, he hoped, work for this more favourably disposed executive. I had a high regard for all three, and had no intention of participating in the game. Unfortunately for my boss he backed the wrong horse; his candidate was given another job and went on up, leaving the reporting levels as before, and the atmosphere supercharged. The effect of all this on the team was not good. It is difficult to deal with this sort of position. If you join in the boss's personal campaigns you join a gang which tends to come off second best. If you do not, you can be accused of disloyalty and suspected even of fifth column work. On balance, it is best never to join a gang. Get on with your job, don't get involved, and let the world make its judgement through what you achieve.

Another difficult situation is where the boss's boss sends for you in the boss's absence and seeks information. This might however, be because Big Boss wants from you what he cannot get from your boss when he is available, or wants to corroborate what he already has. The flattering attention of the Big Boss can encourage you to let off steam and put across your own point of view on this occasion, without the usual filtration system. This can lead to indiscretion and disloyalty. There is no harm in talking freely if you tell him that you will relay the conversation to your own boss on his return, and do so. In a healthy atmosphere the Big Boss will do it anyway, but you never want to establish a link with the Big Boss which leaves your boss wondering what is going on. Your loyalty is to *your* boss, and is not for sale, hire or loan to anyone else.

I have received letters from one of my subordinate's team members which have been highly critical of him, couched in conspiratorial terms which invite me to use the information to clobber his boss. I have always made a point of showing the letter and my reply, which is seldom more than three lines long, to the man's boss and informing the correspondent that I have done so. If he wants to come and see me about a legitimate grievance, then he sees his boss first, and tells him this is what he wants to do.

On one occasion the wife and daughter of a manager two levels below me demanded to see me, so they could put the case on behalf of their breadwinner who had just been transferred to other duties. I discussed the situation with the man's boss, and we agreed to see them together. The wife, who could with advantage have played the Momma in a musical, arrived wearing a great clanking gold charm bracelet which would have broken a lesser woman's arm, and shook this and several beringed fingers at me in the course of a twenty minute diatribe. When I could, I pointed out that I was sure she had come out of loyalty to her husband, but she was not doing him any good, for he had the ability and I hoped the courage to make his own case. I did not propose to take any notice, refer to it again, tell her husband that she had been to see me, or prolong the interview, and they both went away. I never discovered if the poor wretch learned of the incident.

One's strength of character is continually tested in business, when the political decision in order to please the boss's whim, competes with what you believe to be your own better rational judgement. This can happen over the appointment of people and where new products or advertising are concerned. If your boss likes or does not like a product, can he reasonably condition you to launch it or not launch it, to satisfy his view? The Ford Edsel demonstrates that he can, but he is most unwise to set his single judgement, or even that of his friends at the golf club, against the professional research which you must carry out. This has to be done to avoid his, your own, and anyone else's subjective opinion, clouding issues and confusing political pressures and decisions with rational business decisions. Your boss will have ideas and some of them will be good, but if he is human at least half will be non runners. To keep yourself free from political pressures you should establish that all ideas, from whatever source – the petrol pump attendant, the marketing manager, the boss, his wife – will receive the same discipline of objective research and evaluation, and action will be determined as a result of this.

Where the appointment of people is concerned, this is more difficult unless you can demonstrate how they have performed against objectives, or how their track records compare against your expectations. If judgement is to be influenced by blood relationship or external friendship, beware, because the organisation is about to demoralise its good people in an act of cynicism.

Most people in a company are capable of greatly enhanced performances if they are sparked off. To achieve this, the atmosphere must be fair and encouraging. If good, and potentially good, people get the feeling that the virtues of hard work and application are less recognised than the results of devious manipulation, then performance is never extended and most will throttle back.

Significantly, the political atmosphere in a business can change completely, according to the actions and outlook of the man at the top. This atmosphere will take time to improve, as people lower down change their styles for the better, against the obstacle of everyone else knowing how they used to act. It takes less time for the atmosphere to get worse. The pace and direction is set at the top, positively or negatively, and radiates or dissipates through the organisation, depending on the clarity and consistency of the message. It only needs a clear message, the consistent encouragement of the team at all levels to pursue the objectives, and the removal of the few people who would rather make trouble than progress, to transform an atmosphere and charge it with new hope. By the same process it only needs the appointment of one or two unworthy candidates for friendship, personal, or any other reasons, to knock the heart out of those who strive through meritorious work to get on.

11. Women at Work

One must accept that given the obvious physical constraints, there are very few jobs that cannot be done by a competent woman. Most of the existing barriers are erected by men or by women themselves. The reluctance to admit women to the priesthood, for example, has more to do with prejudice and dogma than with any perceived unfittedness for the job, although there will be those to dredge up some good reason or some dreary argument why this is also an issue. In the world league Margaret Thatcher has probably done more to break down barriers erected by tradition than any other woman in recent years, because she has avoided the behavioural and emotional distractions which make many women less able to deal with situations rationally.

If a woman really wants to get on in business then she must leave behind the tears and emotional passions and hatreds when helped or hindered at work. There is no room for the vapours and the shield of femininity when the going gets tough. Either muck in or keep out. Those who can muck in bring a logic which can be creatively stimulating, and often a drive and sense of purpose which puts many a man in the shade. If she has a good brain and knows how to use it, she can provide a sharp prod to the man who is a bit flabby in his thinking and clubbish in his relationships. She may use her womanly charms to lull the patronising and egocentric male into a sense of superiority and then skin him alive in the race for promotion and visible achievement.

Once she uses her charms, however, to distract him and herself, and tries to build a relationship in the business on emotional lines, she is done for. She will be suspect and will start to behave in a way which has little to do with sound judgement. She does not have to be a hard career woman to achieve the balance. What she needs is a commonsense approach to the job in hand, resisting the distraction of mancatching.

There can be few more unwholesome relationships for the rest of the team than when the boss and a woman executive who is part of the team are having an affair. If you have ever lived through the experience of intrigue, innuendo and suspicion you will know how it kicks the bottom out of the integrity that ought to exist between a boss and his subordinates. That he can be stupid enough to compromise himself and jeopardise the objectivity that should exist in the team's view of him is bad enough. Add to this the emotional assessment of the other members of the team and their subordinates, whispered on the pillow, and the team will become preoccupied with the injustice of it all to the exclusion of creative input. This goes much deeper than the jaundiced attitude towards the executive who chases his or another's secretary around the office in the lunch hour. Such behaviour at the place of work will be known throughout the building by nightfall, and if it takes place away from work, it will be known by the end of the week. The more senior the manager who compromises himself in this way, the greater the damage he will do to his relationships, and the more prone to being compromised he will be. If he is supposed to be supplying leadership, he is visible and will invite imitation. To show a weakness of such flaunting proportions at work, of all places, must seriously call into question his judgement and his strength of character.

I have known a situation where the managing director has had the personnel manager as his mistress, and I have seen the same relationship between a personnel director and one of his managers; production director and forewoman; finance director and his boss's secretary – all of these in a variety of companies over the years. The common factor which applies to most of these affairs, and many others too, is that one partner in each has either been significantly unattractive or in some way inadequate in personal relationships. Sometimes both have been afflicted in this way, so it might have something to do with the need to find solace in each other's company which they cannot find at home or in other society.

For every one who pursues an affair at work there will be plenty of others who flirt and talk about it. The usual manipulation of the boss by his secretary, if he must have one – I have always shared a secretary with at least one other – is part of the skill which she learns early on. Plenty of men will respond by giving it back in full measure or maybe allowing themselves to be organised. Gradually the secretary forms a strong and protective relationship towards her boss, which falls well short of any physical involvement, but which puts any subsequent boss into the exacting role of substitute and comparison.

A politician was asked by a heckler at a meeting why, if his party's policies were so perfect, the country was in such a mess. "Can you tell me anything that is really perfect?" he retorted, "My wife's first husband" came a voice from the back.

The sense of ownership and protectiveness by a secretary for her boss can lead to a strong working team. Here the shorthand between them is more than what she writes in her book. She will know his likes and dislikes when travelling and will be able to receive messages without a word being spoken at times. If he does not look up when she comes into the room it could mean he does not want her to break his train of thought; it could also mean he is having a snooze or his tie is caught in his desk drawer. The way she protects him from the outside world, or from others within the business, will usually be a combination of his wishes and her interpretation. If it is too strongly the latter she will be building a barrier between him and those to whom he should be accessible, which will do him no good in time. One should of course, be careful about laying too much at the door of the secretary. The boss must clearly want her to answer the telephone and look up enquiringly at all visitors, or he would not permit her to do it – or would he? Maybe she does quite a bit of his dirty work for him, such as meting out managerial admonitions in his name which he might be reluctant to do himself. The boss's status-needs in having a secretary cause some strange distortions of working behaviour so she can be kept busy. She quite rightly wants an interesting job, and if she is going to spend all her week working for one man she must inevitably want to feel involved in what he does.

The secretary who likes to be busy is either fortunate enough to work for a boss with a varied and complex job, and maybe extra-mural activities which can genuinely keep an efficient hard working woman gainfully occupied all week and every week, or she will contrive to keep herself busy by becoming involved in as much of what he does as possible.

A full-time secretary to an understretched boss is not only a waste of money but counter productive. To show that he can justify her he will write memos, calling forth replies from other understretched executives with full time secretaries, who welcome the game for the same reason. Those secretaries who do have to work hard resent the constant visiting and chatter from those who do not, and the gossip and undercurrents are fed because of it. Generally the happier secretaries are the ones who are fully occupied. If you pay them more money to work for two or more well matched executives; i.e. one who spends a good deal of time away travelling and when he gets back has an avalanche of work to be completed in a short time, and one who is in the office for a greater proportion of his time. then the work load can be spread. This way she always has something to do. She gets paid for it and is in no way diminished because she is not one executive's personal secretary. Indeed if the managing director shows the example and shares his secretary or perhaps someone else's, then a full-time personal secretary becomes an exception to be justified.

Legislation towards equal pay for women has been a major disservice to their employment. Given the choice either to employ a woman or a man at the same cost, then if the man is available and can do the work he will usually get it. He will not have to stay at home when one of the children is sick. He will not become pregnant and need to be guaranteed his job back after it has been held open for many months. It has also meant that a woman is earning a full living wage in her own right. Yet many work to supplement the household income and not to replace the husband as the breadwinner. A marked increase in absenteeism suggests that women will work 3 or 4 days a week to earn their share and then take one or two days off. Absenteeism has increased also among men who see their wives bringing in the same amount of money as themselves, and between them they can work out who has Friday off this week.

I have worked closely with a number of formidable forewomen and supervisors over the years. When a forewoman in charge of a line of girls and a few men is good, she is very good. There is a practical, firm and commonsense quality about the way she does her job, which is all about motivating the team to complete the task each day. This is based on a mixture of firm discipline, – understanding if one of the girls has a genuine problem at home and the whole team rallies round to help, and a fierce championship on behalf of the team in defense of working conditions. Management gets a fair deal, but goes beyond the mark at its peril, and needs the commitment of the forewoman on the production line. A number cultivate a formidable appearance over the years and legends grow up, usually fed by men who have been on the receiving end of a lashing tongue for interfering with her girls, or being a bit slow off the mark in the face of a command. The formidable external package tends to enfold a pillar of the business which gets things done and provides stability.

Good women managers are much fewer and further between. To climb up the tree needs continuity, and many potentially successful woman managers have had their careers interrupted or cut short by marriage and raising a family. The ones who get on are those who are not so diverted. This is inclined to weight the ranks of woman managers with those who are unmarried, who are married and have no children or who were married. Such a cross section is less representative than their male counterparts with whom they must compete for promotion. Also, it usually means that the nearer the top you look the less women there are, hence selection of men and women further down is almost wholly in the hands of men.

The ambitious woman's reaction to this man's world of business is to strive all the harder and this can lead to a certain shrillness and intensity, not to mention the temptation to divert emotionally. This seems to play into the chauvinistic hands of men who like to believe, and seek to prove, that women behave differently to men in business.

Men for the most part have an inbuilt wariness about working with women as equals or superiors. This gives the woman who plans her career coolly and rationally a considerable advantage. The element of surprise and initiative is with her, if she avoids the trap of diversion and of conforming to the expected image of emotional and irrational, eccentric behaviour. It is confusing and bewildering for a chauvinist male who has neatly pigeon-holed his woman colleague to find that she does not behave as he has predicted. And what is more, she seems to be effective in her job. Somehow she avoids entanglements and the loves and hates which are expected to curtail her advance because she is bound to back the wrong horse sometime.

The cry goes up from career women that life is unfair and prejudiced, and to get on you have to be much better than the men who compete for, and get the jobs that they themselves are after. Perhaps there is something in this because those women who do get on are the ones who can avoid emotion and let their ability dominate their activities. The comparison with men, job for job, can be more to do with stability than with ability. How will she respond compared to the way he will respond, at a time of pressure and crisis? What happens to her judgement once a month, and is it right to entrust a large section of the business to a manager subject to unavoidable hormone changes periodically and then menopausally? The belief that it is only women who are subject to moody cycles is of course false, and experts in biorhythms will propound the theory that we are all subject to them.

One successful business man I know, who is now a leading figure in local government, sets store by the sign of the Zodiac under which an applicant for a job was born. He firmly believes this has a fundamental effect upon the man's or woman's makeup and those characteristics will come through in the job. Add your birth sign to your biorhythm and the level of ions in the air according to the weather, and a man has problems enough in contriving consistent and relevant behaviour. This says nothing about his ability and suitability or lack of it for the job. For a woman to add a woman's cycles may indeed give her an added handicap or at least an expected one. This may be all very unfair, especially in those cases where her personality and stability are a good deal more dependable than some of the men who have got what she wanted. Unfair or not, this is what she is up against and she has to battle with it.

Equal pay or not and equal opportunities or not, there are many jobs a woman does better than a man. Bringing up children and running the home, nursing the sick, knitting and dressmaking, typing and data keying, looking after the needy and underprivileged in the community are a few. Teaching small children and writing children's books are two more. There are of course some giants and saints of men in these occupations. The great chefs and dress designers, community care workers and fathers of one parent families, male teachers of the handicapped are perhaps the Margaret Thatchers of their world. Tradition decrees there are jobs for women and jobs for men, and tradition needs a shake up to keep pace with changing attitudes. To keep men or women out of each others' preserves for chauvinist reasons is absurd but this does not mean it will not continue to be done.

There are good reasons why those preserves have been enclosed and among them must be numbered the emotional relevance of the activity to the needs of those who indulge in it. Most men will feel it is cissy to sew womens' dresses. Yet women will regard war as men's work.

Capacity for leadership, however, transcends these barriers with some startling results through history. From Joan of Arc and Boadicea as war leaders to Catherine of Medici,

Catherine the Great of Russia, Queen Elizabeth I, as great Sovereign Chief Executives; plus Florence Nightingale and Golda Meier all with the capacity for inspired leadership of men and women alike by these remarkable women on a world scale. The first woman Pope, Lord Chief Justice, President of the U.S.A. and Chairman of the T.U.C. may be some way off, but who says it cannot happen and indeed who says it should not happen?

The loud lobby in favour of equal opportunity for women would at times give the impression that it speaks for womankind as a repressed and deprived 50% of society. Yet the determination to compete with men at all levels is by no means the wish of the majority. For women to be expected to become less feminine because social convention has reached a certain point in the swing of the pendulum, is to fly in the face of biology and psychology. For every woman who burns her bra and objects to being patronised by courtly manners, there will be a thousand who like a man to hold a door open for her, to give up his seat, raise his hat, stand when she enters the room and take decisions for her, and the blame for them when they don't work out as she had hoped. And all this will be enacted while she is uplifted suitably, attractively and maybe suggestively.

Women are at work continually. Some of them work at being men or as good as men, most of them work at being women and very good they are too . . . . .

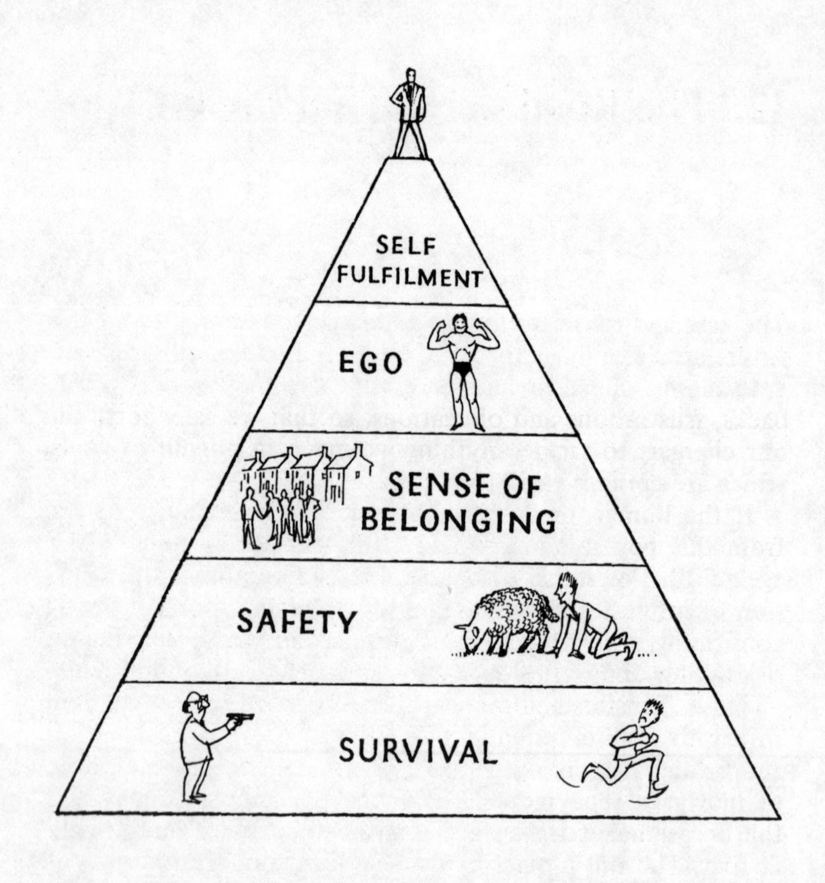
SELF
FULFILMENT
EGO
SENSE OF
BELONGING
SAFETY
SURVIVAL

12. The Road to Self Fulfilment

The zest and relish for life, with its question marks about the future, is keenly experienced at the time of youthful enthusiasm. Idealism and ambition are undimmed by set-backs, frustrations and obligations, so that we sally forth on our chargers to tackle anything we meet, in pursuit of goals which are perhaps vague, but glorious.

If the human brain were not able to adjust and trade off from this position, we should all be off our rockers by the age of 40. For some, of course, life is a continuous progression of interest and achievement, with reality outstripping or confirming such objectives as were set in youth. For many, risk-taking diminishes as family and financial commitments increase. Pension and security become more important than thrust to realise potential. The danger of commitment to action and risk-taking which might shake the delicate fabric of mortgage repayments, HP debts, the annual holiday and the occasional extravagance is avoided, perhaps unwittingly at first. The full impact of the low key, humdrum nature of such an existence comes when it is perceived too late to do anything about it. That is another illusion, for it is seldom too late if the will is there.

Few people ever realise their full potential. This may have much to do with perception of opportunity and not being pointed in the right direction early enough. It has much to do with the image we have of ourselves, forged in childhood by parents and environment. There are those who are encouraged to believe that they are better than they really are in a field unsuited to them – how otherwise do some of the worst speakers become Councillors, politicians or after-dinner 'entertainers'? Or perhaps one member of the family is sat on by the others and made to feel the fool, the inadequate one who subsequently knows his place in society and declines to develop his talent for fear of being crushed or ridiculed.

Most people are good at something, or would be if given half a chance, and it is the pursuit of achievement to the point of satisfaction and recognition which marks the path to fulfilment. Most of us are too busy earning a living to make any money. But if we are also too busy earning a living to realise our potential in any other field, then the humdrum nature of a life of minimal risk is complete, and we wallow in progressive disillusionment until eventually we peter out altogether.

Fortunate is the man or woman who achieves success and fulfilment in the work he or she is paid to do. Much can be done to influence such a happy state. To achieve this in a changing environment requires risk and action which can lead to challenging the status quo of your life. A reluctance to keep pace with this requirement, brought about by the enmeshing commitments of the home and family, brings with it a self-defeating lack of fulfilment in anything, and in work especially.

Business is full of those who cling desperately to what they have and what they do, reluctant to change because it is unknown and threatening, stretching and exacting. Mental retirement can come some ten or fifteen years before physical retirement. Giving up the struggle to push and shove for the new and exciting and settle instead for an acceptable lot, is the portion of many who could do better for themselves and their families if they had the courage to try.

Perhaps there is an element of self-satisfaction in the ones who struggle to succeed. The stress and tension which some fear, and will do almost anything to avoid, is the built-in dynamo of others who feel dull and bored without it. Tension is the stuff of which endeavour is made. Great sporting occasions, record breaking in most fields, trials at law, good television, music and acting – you cannot play a violin, hit a tennis ball, shoot a catapult, a bow and arrow or sleep on a mattress without it.

Perhaps it is because a few can live with it where the majority avoid it, that the few step through the barriers where others stop. A few press on to the brink, to the summit, to the goal mouth, where fainter hearts who want an easier humdrum life of less risk turn away for peace and refuge.

That risk-taking and consequent success or failure means an ability to deal with stress, conflict and tension, must mean that you use more of yourself to strive for greater goals. Whether this constitutes a more likely background for an approach to self fulfilment or not depends upon what fulfils you. But it does seem as people get older that they are inclined to regret the things they have not done more than the things they have. After all, if you have always said no to opportunities as they come along, you can be sure only that you never took them. If you have accepted whatever has come and taken hold of each challenge with guts, vigour and determination you will do more, stretch more and achieve more. If you think you have failed sometimes it is of little importance, for there can be no greater failure than doing very little over a long period and looking back over minimal achievements.

The wife and family for whose peace of mind you are reluctant to take risks are probably much more worried and depressed at the prospect of dull continuity than the prospect of some risky excitement. It cannot be much fun for a family to see their father become duller by the year because of the effect they have upon him.

"What would you be doing, Dad, if we did not exist?"

"Ah I would have taken greater risks and probably achieved great things".

"Well what's stopping you?"

Self fulfilment is a long way up the scale of human needs. In fact it stands at the top of a pyramid described by A.H. Maslow in the forties.

Each step up the pyramid has to be accomplished before the next can be considered.

The most basic need is survival and there are many who make this their prime preoccupation. Refugees, flood and earthquake victims have no time or inclination to consider anything more basic at the first impact and in the chaos immediately following. Perhaps there are relatively fewer people in constant concern at this basic level than in earlier times, and its emergency aspect is the main boost to their numbers. But sheer abject poverty or oppression keeps the numbers at a substantial level.

Next up the pyramid comes safety. Once basic survival can be assured continuity is the next concern. A permanent shelter for one's family, a more certain food and clothes supply and the protection of law and order, enable this climb above the bottom rung to become a reality. The line between survival and safety is a blurred and changing one, for if the crops fail or the political regime changes, then starvation and persecution can take the place of ordered society, however basic.

Next is a sense of belonging. The gregarious nature of the human being in identifying with a tribe or a group, can function when individuals are able to think beyond their own immediate survival. This is the main starting point for most of us in the developed world. The motivating factor is concerned with being accepted and recognised in the society of our choice. The district in which we live or want to live, the golf club, the pigeon fanciers, women's institute, working men's club, army, managers' mess become an important part in our acceptance or rejection, aspirations and fears.

It is only when we have kept up with whatever Joneses we want to match and are safe in our own minds about our place in society, grand or humble as it may be, that we are able to relax sufficiently to pursue the next of the needs which satisfies our egos. There are those whose egos require continual massage and nourishment and which drive them tempestuously to the building of great empires, dynasties and monuments to themselves. Napoleon, Henry Ford, Howard Hughes and their kind. Some are dedicated to the good of mankind such as Lord Nuffield, and some to the destruction of all not conforming to a demented dream, such as Hitler.

On a more usual and reachable scale, to get one's name in the newspaper or to win a prize for onions at a horticultural show, feeds the desire to achieve something a bit special, of which one can be proud, and which spurs the effort and unleashes the adrenalin to show the world you have something which sets you apart. It can be the spur to realisation that you are not the pigeon holed, indexed and predictable package you have believed yourself to be, but that you can break out of the container and form a new shape to your life, which will surprise you as much as it surprises those who thought they had you taped.

Perhaps the final step in the pyramid to self fulfilment depends upon the relationship between the ego drive and the practicality of satisfying it. Few people are wholly self fulfilled at the end of their lives, although there may be moments for most where the glow of satisfaction and achievement take over for a while – maybe a few hours or days – from the struggle to hold on to the place you occupy on the slippery sides of the pyramid. One's position on the pyramid is never constant. Imagine for example Neil Armstrong. His sense of self fulfilment as he stepped on to the surface of the moon must have been staggering and he was 38 at the time. What can he do next to sustain the peak? The answer is nothing. He took up an academic career which initially must have satisfied his need for a sense of belonging, before he could pursue any ego needs in that context, let alone experience again heady self fulfilment.

The fear of slipping down the pyramid must for many inhibit the effort to climb it. But some movement down is inevitable, on the basis that no situation in life is static and if you do not go forward you will surely go back. The less the effort to push forward for fear of falling back, the more certain it is there will be a slide. Cautious determination to avoid taking risks, because of the desire for security for your family, must on this basis be self defeating.

Time of life has very little to do with one's position on the pyramid. Lord Thomson of Fleet took his company into North Sea oil when he was well over 60. Churchill became Prime Minister at an age when most men retire. Pope John 23rd was enthroned at 75 and Adenauer was

Chancellor of West Germany at 80. William Pitt was Prime Minister at 24 and both Schubert and Mozart died in their 30s.

It is never too late to start firing on all cylinders. I have seen incredible transformations in 50 to 55 year olds in business whose horizon had been bounded by the prospect of retirement at 60 or 65, filling the intervening years with the same monotonous work. Then they get the chance to use all their accumulated experience and skill in a way that is relevant and appreciated. Of all the satisfactions in management there are few to compare with the sharing of success, excitement and anticipation. To see this transforming a long serving executive into a thrusting member of a younger, eager pack is especially rewarding.

The use of time, and sheer application, probably distinguish the high achievers from the rest. However you split it up, there are 168 hours in a week and we only have about 3500 – 4000 weeks on this planet – once – unless you believe in reincarnation. We must sleep, and some use up to 50 or 60 hours a week in so doing. We must work and travel to work, which takes up perhaps another 50 hours on average. That leaves 50 or 60 hours a week unaccounted for. Some will use most of it to worry at business problems, which gets the subconscious helping to find solutions of a creative, thrusting nature. Others will switch off from work completely and do something else well. Some will just switch off. The freedom of choice to pursue these or any other courses of action or inaction, is the main distinction of the human being over other species. It must be possible to get some sense of self fulfilment doing nothing, but it is unlikely. The problem is that the realisation that you have not achieved much, or even done much, comes on in life when it is obvious how much time and opportunity has been wasted.

For those who feel a sense of frustration and lack of some self fulfilment, ask yourself what you are waiting for. Why not just get up and DO something about it? One hears frequently of men and women in their 40s and 50s mourning the passing of opportunity, and wishing they could start all over again, because it would be different next time. Well what's the matter with this time, when there are still 20 or 30 years ahead with 50 hours a week to be allocated?

One of the inhibiting factors to this sort of drive up the pyramid, is the reluctance to leave the bosom of the chosen social group into which you are well integrated. To pursue your own ego needs sets you apart and usually on a pedestal, or some visible prominence. As such you are an example to a few and a target for many. Some will admire your energy and enterprise. Most will feel a sense of discomfort at your greater achievement. There will be those who endeavour to belittle it, as a way of transferring the threat away from their own duller performance, and there will be no shortage of those to apply pressure from the touchline, which can make you feel it is antisocial to be successful. Marginal, temporary one upmanship is all part of the social ebb and flow in the welcoming community, but success or involvement beyond that community's horizon sets up a distance. As ego-needs are pursued, the social needs recede to some extent, and it is as well to be sure your family wants to follow that route, or they will be suspended in a limbo between your pursuit of ego satisfaction and a cooling social acceptability, while you are busy doing it.

So it comes back to risk and thrust. Aspirations increase continually in our wasteful and acquisitive society. Today's luxury of which you were so proud when you pipped the neighbours to it, will become tomorrow's yardstick of fitness to belong to that community. Just to keep up in that slot in the pyramid can set up stress and anxiety, if you fear that by not keeping up in material things, you cannot compensate in others. Some of the most valuable members of the community find it hard to make ends meet. They are not motivated by the gadgetty fripperies which seem to give such temporary satisfaction and such permanent anxiety. Instead they pursue interests in which they succeed, give and gain satisfaction. They will be possessed by an inner drive and motivation which the armchair critics will find hard to understand until, and if ever, they too get bitten by some enthusiasm bug, and apply unknown reserves of talent and energy to achievement.

The bored and bitchy are the main enemy of active yet

not very determined people. It is a threat to the indolent and unfulfilled to see success and dedication in others, and they can get some satisfaction from halting some eager thruster in a dust cloud of uncertainty and doubt, through a shrewdly aimed shaft of destruction.

There are plenty of people more at home in the demolition squad than in the construction gang. It really does not matter what they think – the opinions of unsuccessful, unenterprising people are hardly underpinned with much authority. They can be insidious too.

"You must be absolutely exhausted – you will burn yourself out".

"What does your wife think about your being out in the evening?"

"My husband would object if I was not at home to cook him a meal every evening".

Businesses and governments must share some of the responsibility for niche seeking rather than thrusting enterprise. On a new recruit's first day with a company there is discussion about joining the pension fund. The State pervades our lives from cradle to the grave and provides a safety net in which there are already many feet enmeshed. For the State to claim that it knows what is right for the individual, is to proclaim an equality which flies in the face of the evolution of man. Those who painted the map red, provided the great scientific breakthroughs in the last century and brought about the industrial revolution were not governed by the inspiration of State control and moni toring of effort. Centralised supervision of our lives, and the complication of using enterprise in such a society, has not prevented some of the most exciting examples of human achievement in the last 30 years. Freddie Laker for one has demonstrated how an individual with an idea, persistence and enormous tenacity and courage can bring a whole new dimension to other people's lives, in spite of State monopoly and resistance.

To achieve change there first has to be protest. It has been so throughout history and governments; the establishment and the system have usually been against it when it starts. It is the energy and determination of those who would bring it about which sees it through. So look around.

URGENT

13. Working Habits

If you want to get on, the nine to five mentality will not help. Events do not conveniently fall between those hours, particularly if you travel, entertain, buy companies and negotiate deals. Other people's time clocks will also determine the best time of day or night when you can obtain the desired degree of responsiveness for successful dealings with them

You do not need to be a workaholic to succeed in business although many who do are just this. They are not the easiest bosses to work for. The hours they put in help to induce a sense of guilt and omission among those who lead a more normal life. It sets up strains at home if nothing can be planned domestically because of unscheduled meetings, late finishes and early starts. At times of particular pressure and crises such involvement can be justified, but it is not conducive to building a team of well integrated managers if they are continually having to avoid all out of office activity or cancel it at short notice.

There is also no point in holding breakfast meetings with people who are incoherent until mid-morning. At the other end of the day, if a man has promised to take his wife out to dinner, he is not going to be receptive to digging into an open ended session because the boss has nothing to do that night, or no other interests besides his work.

Working habits go much deeper than presence at the

place of work or at some other work-connected venue. Those who say they switch off as soon as they leave the office are either not going to get very far, or are being less than honest. If you have business problems, and who in business has not, then the continual churning in your mind, sleeping on them, picking them up and wrestling with them until you have the solution, is all part of the frontal attack on the obstacles that stand between a manager and his goals. That does not mean that you have to take home piles of work and lock yourself away each evening and at weekends. It probably does mean you will have to be brought back to the thread of domestic or social chatter wafting around you while your mind has been dwelling on a problem.
"You never listen to a word I say"
"I told you last week . . . ."
must be fairly universal accusations in the homes of executives. It is not unreasonable for the family to want to share their man with the business which absorbs so much of his time and energy. But one contribution a family can make to the pressured breadwinner is to give him a chance to think at times, without domestic clatter taking over from office clatter the moment he walks through the door.

It is possible to think and work anywhere. Those who need complete quiet and solitude or a particular room or venue are giving themselves an obstacle course, or maybe a set of excuses to be cleared before they can start. Jane Austen would write on scraps of paper on the corner of a mantlepiece in a crowded room oblivious of the noise and clamour around her. She did not always write like this but she could and did if the mood took her.

The way in which your boss works will be unique to him. I have worked for men whose offices have been isolated havens of seldom interrupted peace at one extreme, and hives of seemingly constant activity at the other, with a regular stream of callers, the telephone ringing constantly and piles of paper on show. Their working style has not been easily related to effectiveness. Although those who seem to be most in touch, and who achieve most, tend to be the ones who welcome contact and have the sort of accessibility which places the minimum of obstacles in the way of it.

There is something unreal and unnerving when the boss's tempo and detachment from the bustle and pressures in which you have to operate, or perhaps in which you choose to operate, is markedly different from your own. The change of tempo is more likely to be experienced in service functions than with your line boss who after all is part of the same battle. History is full of the frustrations of the busy, pressured field commander coming up against detached complacency or ignorant judgement and half baked unhelpful criticism, from those who can indulge in the luxury of being spectator to the real action.

Alfred Sloan when President of General Motors, is supposed to have said that for the first 90 minutes of each morning he would only permit two people to interrupt him. One was the President of the United States and the other was his wife. "The President does not call very often and my wife knows better".

A manager's main stock in trade is acquiring and considering information; then applying the result through people. Without information and without relating to people he can do nothing. His main task in his working habits must therefore be geared to these two requirements. Reading and communicating, seeing for yourself and personal contact take up the greater part of business life. Finding time to read and the opportunity to think has to be snatched amid the daily pressures and contact with your team. This can be done effectively when others are not around to interrupt, and early in the morning before they arrive, or later in the evening after they have gone, are good options. Train journeys and sitting at airports provide essential interludes to clear the backlog of the thick reports and background information, which tend to get put aside in favour of the work that can be squeezed in between meetings, telephone calls and other interruptions.

I once worked out that if I attended every relevant course and conference that came across my desk, I would be out of the country for the equivalent of 5 weeks in the year, and at home based centres for the equivalent of a further 10 weeks. Also if I read everything sent to me from whatever source it would amount to the equivalent of three full length novels a week. A minister in the British Government has the equivalent of a full length novel each day to absorb.

Those who cope successfully with a heavy and varied work load have the ability to concentrate the mind on the issue in hand, to the exclusion of other problems, and to deal with it decisively. Despatching business, making decisions, solving problems and reaching the people with, or to acquire the information you want, is the key to devouring a work mountain which would be quite impossible for an indecisive procrastinator. Such an action minded executive will also have a profound effect on those who work for him. If he processes the contents of his desk top within 24 hours of receipt, he will set a pace which will jerk others into getting on with solving their problems. A meeting with a subordinate should always yield some results for both. Decisions made, plans agreed or obstacles removed. If a subordinate comes with a list of points to be discussed, he wants, or should want, to depart with the majority of those points sorted out. Maybe others will have been added but that is progress.

The 'Oh, to hell with it' attitude which is the death of energetic enterprise in a business, usually has its roots in the boss responding to initiatives or requests for decisions by asking for a paper to be written, (yet another one) or saying he is too busy to deal with the matter. "Can't you come back in a week's time, or maybe a month and we'll discuss it then". Contrast this with the decisive boss who makes up his mind on all matters in his decision area then and there, or possibly asks twenty-four hours to sleep on it and then decides. Furthermore if the subordinate is blocked by a colleague or another part of the business, the boss who reaches for the telephone and unblocks the problem then and there is likely to get, and is entitled to expect, speedy action from his subordinates in getting on with their agreed programmes and producing results.

You need to be sure of your ground with this sort of boss. If you just want a gripe session about all the frustrations and the problems, beware. You should make it clear that is what you are after, although how welcome you will be is perhaps doubtful. It is unnerving when, in mid gripe, the boss picks up the telephone and confronts the cause of your frustration then and there with the problem. This makes for a healthy open atmosphere in the business if you are pushing for action. If you are not then what are you trying to do?

There is no substitute for personal contact with your own staff. They like to know for whom they are working. What do you look like – are you human – how do you react to them and are you in touch with their problems? It gives a quite different perspective listening to those at the end of the communication line, and is a source of amazement and shock, when you hear a distortion of policy or a strange account of events which you know to be wrong, coming from those who believe it to be fact. Giving the message yourself, in much the same terms from top to bottom, including the Trades Union representatives, at least ensures the transmission of facts and figures is carried out even handedly. This leaves much less opportunity for distortion by confusion or otherwise, makes for understanding and as a result a greater interest throughout the business. It is as wrong to flinch from communicating good news for fear of an instant demand for more money, as it is to hold back on bad news for fear of sagging morale. If the information is set in the correct background of the targets the company has to achieve to stay alive and flourish, the 'goodness' or the 'badness' of the news will be understood in a way which flattens out the more prominent peaks and valleys.

The majority of your work force should see you at least once a year, and at least half of those who work for you should see you at least every six months, or more frequently depending on the size of the business. When business is tough it is important to be seen out there amongst it, joined in the battle and leading from the front. When results are good, it is only fair to share your own relief and elation with those without whose efforts it could not have been achieved.

Customers and suppliers like to see the boss, and your own staff can gain some benefit from this if they can work up a deal before an important visit of the brass. Sir John

Cohen, founder of Tesco Stores, used to wear a tie pin which had YCDBSOYA inscribed on it. He relished being asked to explain that it stood for You Can't Do Business Sitting On Your Arse. The big corporations tend to inhibit individualistic behaviour in favour of an unmemorable conformity. To be a good company man becomes the aim, and the more unexpected and eccentric aspects of management and leadership tend to be frowned upon in many companies. Perhaps the message has to be overstated to get it across. The message can be a bit larger than life, and couched in language which is remembered, even though it might be frowned upon by the more conventional. They perhaps believe that withholding their approval will put them in good odour with the Establishment, whilst the majority will have got the message in a form that means something for once.

Leaders have endless variations in their stamp of individualism. General Sir Thomas Picton led his troops at the Battle of Waterloo clad in hunting attire complete with top hat, and added an umbrella for good measure. There is a quite startling photograph of Alfred Krupps with his executives. Each is dressed almost identically in a dark suit, stiff collar and tie and has a triangle of white handkerchief protruding about two inches from the breast pocket, except for Alfred Krupps who has no handkerchief on view at all. The line between being readily identifiable, and drawing attention to oneself in an absurd way, is a fairly thin one. A prominent tattoo for example, applied in a moment of youthful irresponsibility and in doubtful taste, is hardly an asset as you climb the tree. Although there is an apparently true story of an Admiral who was seen standing stark naked in his cabin, by a Lieutenant bearing a message, and on his back was tattooed a hunt in full cry, going from north to south with the fox about to go to earth.

Some managers cultivate strange ideas about time off and holidays. One I knew never took a holiday but instead had every Friday off. He felt he was a martyr giving the firm a level of service which was overdue for recognition. In fact 52 Fridays added up to some 2½ times his entitlement of working days off per year. It did not say much for his boss that he was able to get away with it for some years. In due course he was told he must take his holidays like everyone else, which had an interesting effect on the performance of his team on Fridays.

Work study experts have identified how little real work is done per hour by the average office sitter. There is plenty of rustling of paper, telephoning for one's personal benefit, looking for files, doodling, getting up for a cup of coffee or to chat with someone else. The amount of work which one can get through in an hour of concentrated, undistracted application is enormous. But it needs the discipline of anchoring oneself firmly to a single spot and tackling everything before you in the order in which it comes. The temptation to get on with the simple things and put the brain stretchers aside is denied, and the mind tears into problems and work with hunger. The same amount of work can be quite easily spread over a day or two with sufficient interruptions, visiting and meetings.

For some, a two week holiday spreads over six weeks. During the first two, no initiatives can be undertaken because there is all the preparation of going away. Then on return there is a two week pick up from the two week holiday. It should be possible to gather the threads from a two weeks absence in two hours of concentrated work, preferably before other people arrive for work. 7 a.m. to 9 a.m. on the morning of return can see you well informed by the start of most people's working day. By 10 a.m. you will probably have forgotten you have had a holiday at all.

There is appalling waste of intelligent people's time and brains in those who seek to do the minimum at work consistent with just acceptable performance. The clock watching, weekend seeking, unfulfilled and bored executive is not doing himself or his firm any favours. A company has no more right to insult the intelligence of its executives by permitting poor performance in undemanding jobs, than the executive has in poor application of his effort to the detriment of the firm.

Good working habits start with getting used to working, and good work for an executive contains a measure of innovation and initiative which takes the task of earning a living from a humdrum playing out of necessity, to a stimulating creation of a new shape for the job and the personal satisfaction of success.

One avoids any general exhortation to physical exercise and clean living. Some of the most alert and successful men in business smoke, drink and seem never to take any organised exercise. Indeed the keep fit enthusiast could well ask himself what he is keeping fit for. To be fit to jog five miles a day makes you fit to jog five miles a day, if you do not drop dead in the process. The argument is that the glow of well being, or is it more of self righteousness, helps the alertness of the brain and the energy you put into the job. If it switches you on then by all means do it, but never underestimate those who retain robust health and vitality in a less tormented frame. While the jogger is proclaiming his virtue to anyone who has the time to listen, he should not be surprised if others less self-preoccupied are getting on with the job and achieving more as a result.

It takes discipline and imagination to work effectively. Grinding routine is often the substitute for imagination as one gets caught up in the sameness of it all, and persuades oneself of the virtues of hard work whether or not it is productive, or even necessary.

14. Men or Mice?

The more recognisable sort of courage which gives a man respect, and perhaps a sense of self-effacing self-respect, is performance in the face of physical danger, illness or disability. Yet the everyday courage needed to cope with the continual pitiless grind of business, of earning a living, keeping a home and family and achieving life's goals, is every bit as demanding, drawn out and unrelenting as it is.

Many just cannot take it and give up or opt out. They seek the quieter life and less aggravation, and try to spin out time until the pressures are off them and they can fade into retirement out of the race.

Nettle grasping and risk taking are not a noted characteristic of the timid, and failure in this area is bound to affect performance adversely. Hence pressures build, failures accumulate and refuge is sought, so that one adopts a defensive frame of mind clinging ever more desperately to what one has, and accepting with growing fatalism progressively lower personal goals. It is not difficult to think yourself into a frame of mind where fear of losing what you have, is more preoccupying than determination to pursue what you do not have, and what you want. It takes perhaps some great liberating event to switch the balance. For example, the event which you fear most becomes reality, and then you have to do something to pull yourself up and start fighting, rather than defending and slipping. If you can fight when disaster has struck, how about trying it before it strikes and the chances are it never will.

One can argue that those who display courage under fire never knew they had it in them before the guns opened up, and therefore those in business who need to fight and do so when disaster strikes, would not be moved to it until this hostile environment is upon them. That however depends upon one's frame of mind. If your attitude to life is one of acceptance of fate, reluctance to question and preparedness to go with the tide or the perceived wishes of authority, then you are a mouse and will be unlikely to fight except in extremis, and even then with apologies for causing a disturbance.

The courage to succeed is the courage never to be defeated however thwarted, opposed or disapproved. This presupposes that there is some thrust and dynamism in you, apparent or latent. There is something to be switched on in most people, unusual or eccentric though it may be. The pursuit of this potential has to withstand discouragement or lack of enthusiasm from those who do not understand it, would rather not be involved in the discomfort of progress or who are generally negative or mischievous. In the face of hostility and discouragement the mice scuttle. The men get even more determined and find new ways of overcoming yet another obstacle placed in their path. The determination to achieve what you have established as your goal, requires sensible assessment of time scale and continued relevance, to counterbalance too great a reliance on a pig headed rush in the face of all advice and caution. It can take as much courage to change course in the light of events or advice, as to thrust single mindedly for a goal in the first place.

Self preservation through sickening back pedalling, compromise, yielding and ducking to pressure has to fail in time, if only in its build up of self contempt that you did not have the guts to follow your hunch, or stick with your convictions. Rationalisation as 'political expediency' for every craven retreat tends to wear thin when your accumulated retreats leave you in some unexpected backwater or outside the gate. A poor contributor with little to show for commitment to the company's goals although his behaviour conforms, his service is long and contacts many, is likely to be vulnerable at a time of rapid change of environment. Adaptability is an asset if it is geared to the pursuit of new goals. If it is just another bout of survival or chameleon camouflage against a new background, then it is a further risky stagger towards eventual release or discovery. And what sort of life is that? You look back at all the things you did not do to preserve what you had, and then lost it when you could have been getting stuck into new initiatives or leaving your mark on what you had touched.

Effective and decisive action has to compete with negative delay and inertia. The pain caused by creating anything must include an element of destruction. There are many who dislike the process and their reasons will vary, but there are few who do not enjoy the resulting improvement and the success it brings. To be amongst those who cause improvements to happen, and thus among those who win success, you have to have a cutting edge which remains sharp and active. One can afford to be patient with those who are prepared to learn and change, and bringing this change about is among the most satisfying aspects of business. But for the weak and destructive who drag on the brake and undermine one's efforts to thrust, there can be no such feelings.

The pioneers in any field are usually armed with a conviction that what they are doing is worthwile and important, certainly in their own eyes. They have a destiny to fulfil or a faith to proclaim, a set of objectives to obtain or a discovery to make and later develop. Their determination is their shield against the wingeing of the faint hearted and negative. In business one has to pursue conviction with similar determination, but it has to start with conviction. Too few executives believe in anything firmly enough to risk shaking the status quo. They fear that if they stick a head up above the undergrowth it will be shot off, so they keep a low profile and scuttle about among the familiar shrubs which provide cover from the light.

The frustration of such an existence manifests itself in a sub culture of muttering and rumbling out of earshot of those who can challenge. Safe opposition to be immediately denied with a protestation of loyalty if confronted, tends to become the outlet for those who have not the guts or the capacity to make their voices heard in pursuit of progress.

There is never any shortage of reasons why action should not or cannot be taken. The cry that change takes time, must be gradual and it's all so difficult, will be believed, until someone takes the initiative and does the very things the organisation has been debating. Change certainly takes time, but it takes even longer if you do not start the process with a view to completing the relevant phase by a given date. It is not surprising that decent people flinch from taking hurtful action. The health and integrity of an organisation depends upon a sense of human values which excites rather than threatens, and which encourages rather than suppresses. But the future of the majority is often dependent upon decisive action which affects a minority. At such a time it is no help to excuse inaction by high flown ideals.

Preoccupation with the fear of what might happen if it all went wrong, is usually quite futile and while you are thinking about it, the chances are that it is going wrong. Wholehearted commitment to goals will be much more likely to achieve them than any other attitude, and although the result may not be everything you had desired, it will be very much better than you had feared.

The power of the mind to influence events cannot be doubted. If your attitude is positive and determined, you will see things quite differently from the pessimistic and hopeless. The two shoe salesmen in Africa demonstrate this. One got off the boat, took one look and cabled home:-
"Situation hopeless – no one wears shoes over here – returning home at once".
The other sent a cable:-
"Opportunity unlimited – send 1000 pairs at once".
The determination to face every situation that arises, in the belief that it can be overcome or turned to advantage, is always helped by the realisation that you are competing in an arena with other human beings. They are faced with the same set of problems although they may see them differently. And what have these other human beings got? They will have been born like the rest of us, and have the same potential human hangups, and capacity to make

something of their lives or wallow around and eventually sink. Why should we believe they have an automatic right to succeed any more than us? Who are they to induce any sense of inadequacy in fellow human beings? So clear the road. . . . .

Years ago when I was a young trainee van salesman I was sent into a very difficult customer by the regular man by whom I was being trained. She greeted me with a torrent of abuse and insults in front of her customers and I emerged looking bewildered and shattered.

"What's the matter Son?" – the salesman found difficulty in hiding his mirth.

"That woman . . . . I went in and before I could say a word, she started shouting and screaming . . . ."

"Look" he said "there are 50 million people in Britain and you are bound to find one silly cow"

It was said of Churchill that he was like a rubber ball – the harder you jumped on him the higher he bounced. When the going is tough and you wonder what is going to hit you next, you need some anchor to hold on to. You never, ever want to give up. Life is a fight from start to finish and it requires stamina and courage, resilience and singlemindedness if you are to be a man.

Recent and forthcoming titles also published by

Scope Books

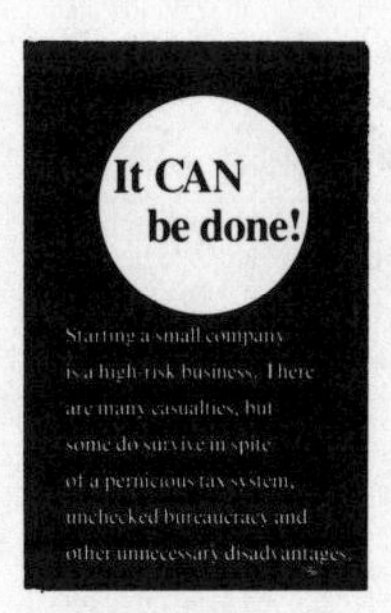

It CAN be done!

21 studies of small businesses, most of them started from nothing, often in garages or back bedrooms, which have "come good" and now make high profits.

Edited by John M. Ryan *Publ. 19.4.79*
0 900619 00 9 (HB) **£4.95**
0 906619 01 7 (PB) **£2.75**

The Entrepreneurs

A close and careful study of four contemporary businessmen who have built up great empires.

by Elizabeth Hennessy *Publl. 12.3.80*
0 906619 04 1 (HB) **£6.50**
0 906619 03 3 (PB) **£4.20**

Investing to Survive the '80s

Inside Information for Businessmen and Investors

Anyone with spare cash should read this book — from the big investor to the housewife, from the dedicated collector to the dedicated gambler. All you have always wanted to know about all types of investment is covered.

by Malcolm Craig *Publ. 30.4.80*
0 906619 06 8 (Hardback only) . . . **£5.95**

Scope Books
3 Sandford House, Kingsclere,
Newbury, Berkshire RG15 8PA